LEARNING & MEMORY

The Brain in Action

MARILEE SPRENGER

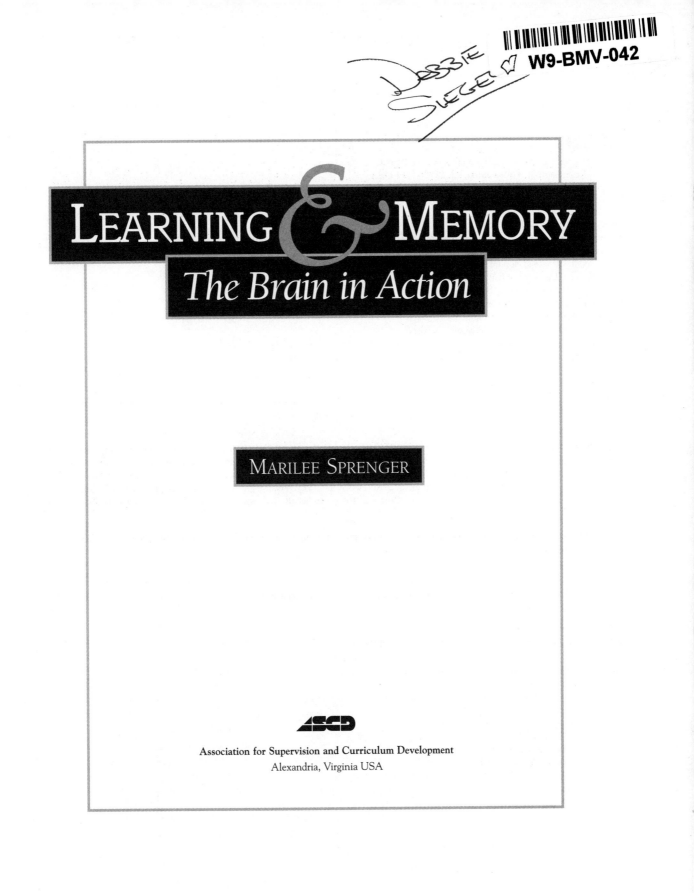

ASCD

Association for Supervision and Curriculum Development
Alexandria, Virginia USA

Association for Supervision and Curriculum Development
1703 N. Beauregard St. • Alexandria, VA 22311-1714 USA
Telephone: 1-800-933-2723 or 703-578-9600 • Fax: 703-575-5400
Web site: http://www.ascd.org • E-mail: member@ascd.org

Gene R. Carter, *Executive Director*
Michelle Terry, *Associate Executive Director, Program Development*
Nancy Modrak, *Director, Publishing*
John O'Neil, *Director of Acquisitions*
Joyce McLeod, *Development Editor*
Julie Houtz, *Managing Editor of Books*
Carolyn R. Pool, *Associate Editor*
Charles D. Halverson, *Project Assistant*
Gary Bloom, *Director, Design and Production Services*
Karen Monaco, *Senior Designer*
Tracey A. Smith, *Production Manager*
Dina Murray, *Production Coordinator*
John Franklin, *Production Coordinator*
Valerie Sprague, *Desktop Publisher*
Joseph Pomerance, *Proofreader*
Robert Land, *Indexer*

Printed in the United States of America.

September 1999 member book (pcr). ASCD Premium, Comprehensive, and Regular members periodically receive ASCD books as part of their membership benefits. No. FY00-1.

ASCD Stock No. 199213
ASCD member price: $17.95   nonmember price: $21.95

Library of Congress Cataloging-in-Publication Data
Sprenger, Marilee, 1949-
     Learning and memory : the brain in action / Marilee Sprenger.
     p. cm.
  Includes bibliographical references and index.
  ISBN 0-87120-350-2 (pbk.)
  1. Learning, Psychology of. 2. Learning—Physiological aspects.
3. Brain. 4. Memory. 5. Teaching. I. Title.
  LB1057 .S67 1999
  370.15'23—dc21
                                                      99-6551
                                                      CIP

04 03 02 01 00 99   10 9 8 7 6 5 4 3 2 1

Learning and Memory: The Brain in Action

Preface and Acknowledgments · · · · · · · · · · · · · · · · · v

1   Losing Your Mind: The Function of Brain Cells · · · · ·   1

2   Chicken Soup for the Brain:

    The Effects of Brain Chemicals · · · · · · · · · · · · ·   15

3   Pieces and Parts: The Anatomy of the Brain · · · · · · ·   30

4   Strolling Down Memory Lanes: Memory

    and Storage Systems · · · · · · · · · · · · · · · · · ·   45

5   Where Is Wally? Locating Memories in the Brain · · · ·   57

6   The Path Most Traveled: Semantic Memory

    Instructional Strategies · · · · · · · · · · · · · · · ·   64

7   The Lanes Less Traveled: Instructional Strategies for

    Episodic, Procedural, Automatic, and

    Emotional Memory · · · · · · · · · · · · · · · · · ·   72

8   Producing the Evidence: Assessment That Mirrors

    Instructional Strategies · · · · · · · · · · · · · · · ·   81

9   Frequently Asked Questions · · · · · · · · · · · · ·   93

    Glossary ·   103

    Bibliography ·   106

    Index ·   108

    About the Author · · · · · · · · · · · · · · · · · · ·   114

Dedication

To Scott, Josh, and Marnie
for their endless love, patience, and support

Preface and Acknowledgments

In the late 1980s, I realized that my students weren't learning as easily or eagerly as they had in previous years. For some reason, they were changing—and my techniques and attitudes were not. My first approach to this dilemma was to get them to "change back," to fit my teaching model. I finally discovered that the only person I could change was myself. So I started searching for information. I took classes on discipline, parenting, self-esteem, and music. I researched learning styles, talked to child psychologists, and read anything I could about the brain.

In 1992 I signed up for a five-day graduate class with brain "guru" and author Eric Jensen. During that week I discovered my new passion—the human brain. Eric asked if I wanted to travel with him and be trained in presenting workshops on brain-compatible strategies for teaching. I was reluctant to leave my husband, Scott, and our children for part of the summer. I was born and raised in Peoria, Illinois, attended Bradley University in Peoria, and married my high school sweetheart. The thought of traveling with a stranger from California was frightening for this Midwestern woman. So I declined.

After watching me pout for several days, my very understanding and supportive husband said the words that would change my life: "If you don't go, nothing will ever change." I called Eric and asked if I could still join him. He said yes. After training with him that summer, I began my own research and designed other classes on brain research and teaching strategies. I have been training educators in practical, brain-compatible teaching strategies every summer and available weekend since then.

My research on the brain continued. I began to see what a powerful factor the research had become in my classroom and in my personal life. Getting up in the morning and going to school became a joy for me once again. I realized the importance of this information and began teaching my students how their brains worked, so they could become better learners. I found that my students looked forward to growing new dendrites and strengthening their synapses!

Learning and memory eventually became my focus. As I spoke at state and national conferences, classroom teachers inspired me. Their excitement at learning this new information was infectious. The application of the research to my classroom experience offered tangible evidence that these strategies could make a difference.

I decided to put it all on paper. Although nothing appears to remain constant in this field, I wanted teachers to know two things: (1) the brain has everything to do with learning, and (2) the more we know about brain science, the easier it will be to make the hundreds of decisions each day that affect our students.

It took almost a year to put this book together. Scott became my personal editor until ASCD turned me over to Joyce McLeod, whose writing and editing expertise guided me through this publishing experience. I had self-published two previous books, but in this situation I required guidance and support. Joyce offered both.

I am grateful to those experts who showed me the way into this exciting field of brain research. Robert Sylwester has answered many of my questions through the years. Pat Wolfe has encouraged my work and been a wonderful role model. Science writer Janet Hopson graciously answered my e-mail queries; and Eric Chudler, a neuroscientist, has inspired both my middle school students and my graduate students as we study the brain. His wonderful Web site, *Neuroscience for Kids* (http://weber.u.washington.edu/~chudler/neurok.html), and his tireless patience in answering our questions added a great deal to our learning. I am also grateful for my friends who listened to all my "brain talk" during the years, especially Glenn Posmer.

The knowledge I gained allowed me to change my approach to teaching in such a powerful way that I would like to share it with other teachers, administrators, and anyone else who is curious about how the brain works and who is interested in making a difference in the lives of students.

MARILEE SPRENGER
Peoria, Illinois
September 1999

1

Losing Your Mind:
The Function of Brain Cells

It is bridge night, and some friends and I are talking about a mutual friend's new baby. As we reminisce, the births of my own children come to mind. I remember the middle-of-the-night dash to the hospital, the pain, the excitement, and the exhaustion. There are some things you just never forget.

One of my bridge friends interrupts my thoughts and asks, "How much did your babies weigh?"

I reach back into my memory of Josh's birth and that exciting day. I open my mouth to speak and say, "Josh weighed 7 pounds . . . umm, 7 pounds . . ." My brain just isn't functioning correctly. I know the answer to this like I know my own name. I own this information. A mother should never forget this stuff. What did he weigh? The embarrassment is overwhelming, so I quickly say, "Oh, yes, Josh weighed 7 lbs. 5 oz." It is a lie. What in the world is wrong with me?

What's happening to my brain when I can't recall an important fact?

On the way home I remembered Josh's birth weight. I was so relieved. I thought I was really losing my mind. Was I losing it? No, not in the sense that I would no longer be able to function. Why couldn't I remember Josh's birth weight? That question has many different answers. Let's examine the brain to find out how it works. Then answering questions about our memories will be easier.

At birth the brain weighs about one pound. By age 18 to 20, it weighs about three pounds.

Brain Cells

The brain is a fascinating organ. Like the rest of the body, it is composed of cells; but brain cells are different from other cells. Our discussion focuses on two types of brain cells: *neurons* and *glial cells*. Although the brain has many other types of cells, these are the ones most involved in learning.

1

Neurons

The brain cell that gets much attention is the neuron. *Neuron* simply means "nerve cell." Until recently, it was believed that the brain could not generate new neurons. Recent research shows that in one area, the hippocampus, there is evidence of new cells (Kinoshita, 1999). Before birth the brain produces about 250,000 neurons per minute. At birth, we have about 100 billion neurons, and although we maintain that number, the neurons may lose their connecting powers (Diamond & Hopson, 1998). If neurons are not used at appropriate times during brain development, their ability to make connections dies. Neuroscientists call this process "neural pruning." So, yes, we are all losing our minds!

However, you don't need to panic about those lost connections. The ones that you have left can take care of anything you need to know or learn for the rest of your life. Some research implies that we use from 1 to 20 percent of our brain. However, we actually use all of our brain, but not all of its processing power (Chudler, 1998). The miracle of the brain is that it is built for continual learning.

What is learning, and how does it occur in the brain? Neuroscientists define learning as two neurons communicating with each other. They say that neurons have "learned" when one neuron sends a message to another neuron (Hannaford, 1995). Let's examine the process.

A neuron has three basic parts: the *cell body,* the *dendrites,* and the *axon* (see figure 1.1). Your hand and forearm are "handy" representations of a neuron. The cell body can be compared to the palm of your hand. Information enters the cell body through appendages called *dendrites,* represented by your fingers. Just as you wiggle your fingers, your dendrites are constantly moving as they seek information. If the neuron needs to send a message to another neuron, the message is sent out through the axon. Your wrist and forearm represent the axon. When a neuron sends information down its axon to communicate with another neuron, it never actually touches the other neuron. The message has to go from the axon of the sending neuron to the dendrite of the receiving neuron by "swimming" through a space called the *synapse.* As the neurons make connections, the brain is growing dendrites and strengthening the synapses. (See figure 1.2.)

If we have 100 billion neurons in our head, they must be very small. Imagine this: 30,000 neurons can fit on the head of a pin. That's impressive, but there's more. Each neuron may be linked with another 5,000 to 10,000 neurons. The brain has about one quadrillion neural connections (Wolfe, 1996). That's a lot of communication going on inside our heads! The process of neurons talking to each other is electro-chemical: the

The brain cells involved in learning are neurons and glial cells.

At birth we have about 100 billion neurons.

The brain sends messages through its neurons.

Learning occurs when two neurons communicate.

As neurons make more connections, or "learn," the brain gets heavier.

Figure 1.1. A Neuron

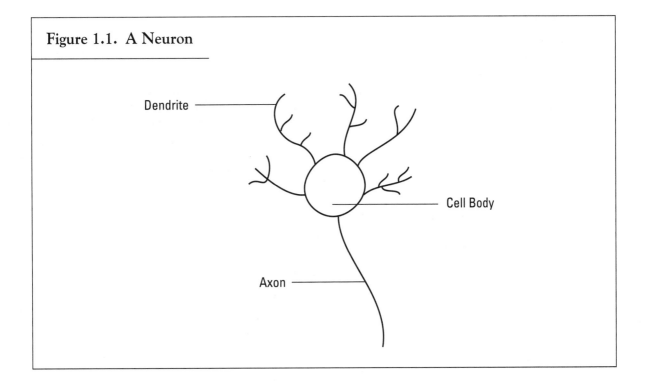

Dendrite

Cell Body

Axon

action within the neuron is electrical, but the message becomes chemical as it travels between neurons. The chemicals are called *neurotransmitters*. Chapter 2 provides more information about neurotransmitters.

Think about a small child's first experience when his mother points out a red bird and tells the child, "That's a red bird. It's called a cardinal." The child attempts to repeat the word. "Cawdnal. Bood." The child's brain has made a connection. A few neurons are now talking to each other about birds. If the child watched as the bird flew out of the tree, he may have the connecting neurons of bird-cardinal-fly. The next time he sees a cardinal, his brain will make those connections again. This time the neurons may connect faster, because when neurons learn or practice information, they become more efficient at connecting.

Neurons are stored in columns in the upper portion of the brain called the *neocortex* (Sylwester, 1995). The child might make other connections related to the cardinal. If he sees geese flying south, he might add that to the bird-cardinal-fly connection. From there, he might add a butterfly or an airplane.

This chain of neurons is called a *neural network*. The more often the brain accesses the network, the stronger the connections become. Those synapses, or spaces, become stronger as well. As these neurons are

Children make connections easily.

The more frequently a neural network is accessed, the stronger it becomes.

Figure 1.2. How Neurons Communicate

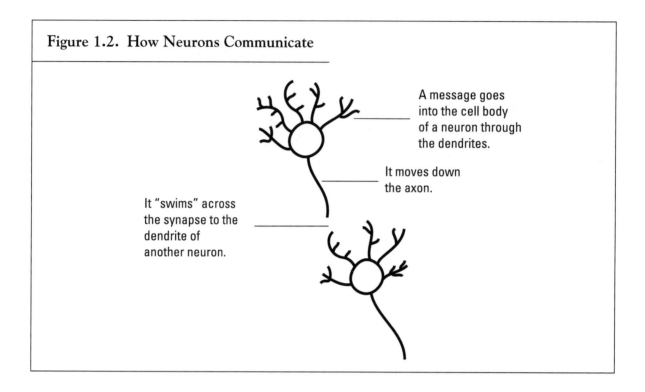

A message goes into the cell body of a neuron through the dendrites.

It moves down the axon.

It "swims" across the synapse to the dendrite of another neuron.

Neural networks begin as rough paths and eventually become more like superhighways.

repeatedly "fired," that is, talk to each other, the dendrites and axons become accustomed to the connections, and the connections are easier to make. Compare this to a path in the woods. The first time you create a path, it is rough and overgrown. The next time you use it, it is easier to travel because you have previously walked over the weeds and moved the obstacles. Each time thereafter, it gets smoother and smoother. In a similar fashion the neural networks get more and more efficient, and messages travel more swiftly.

Researchers are currently exploring an important theory called *long-term potentiation* (LTP). LTP suggests that every time a neuron fires information across a synapse, the memory of that information is encoded exponentially. That means the information is learned multiple times each time it is practiced. The signal has changed the potential of the receiving neuron, and it now has the potential to learn faster (Fitzpatrick, 1996).

The brain makes neural connections at an enormous rate during the early years.

During the first year of life, the brain makes neuronal connections at an enormous rate. Some scientists say that after the first two years, the brain never again learns as much or as quickly. What is happening during this time? The brain is first wiring the infant up to his body. It is making the connections for movement, sight, and sound (Begley, 1997). The baby is also making connections with his primary caretaker. Using his own sounds and movements, the infant communicates with those who are meeting his needs. He begins to recognize voices as well as the expression in those voices. The baby rapidly learns which sounds will get him the desired attention.

Because the brain is so immature at birth, it takes another 18 to 20 years to complete the wiring. We are a social culture, and each individual must "wire up" to a specific culture and society (Sylwester, 1997a). Specific brain areas develop at their own rates.

As social creatures, we must "wire up" to our society.

Glial Cells

The second type of brain cell, the glial cell, is just beginning to get the attention it deserves. Glial cells are nurturing cells for the neurons. *Glial* means "glue," and neuroscientists had good reasons for this name. Glial cells first assist in the migration of neurons during fetal brain development. Their fibers act like ropes for the neurons to hold onto as they make their way through the brain (Kunzig, 1998). The glial cells feed and do the housekeeping for the neurons, almost attaching themselves to the neurons to keep them nourished. The more often the brain uses neurons, the more glial cells it needs. Indeed, when researchers dissected Albert Einstein's brain, they found an extraordinary collection of glial cells in a specific area of his brain. They concluded that this area in Einstein's brain showed more possible use than the same area in any other brain ever studied (Diamond, 1996).

Glial cells are brain cells that nurture the neurons.

An abundance of glial cells in a particular area of the brain indicates that area has been used often.

Unlike neurons in most areas of the brain, glial cells can reproduce, so we can have as many as our brain needs. Communication remains fast and easy because these glial cells work and nurture the neurons.

Myelin

Another substance that neuroscientists are studying is *myelin*. This fatty substance coats the axons of neurons (see figure 1.3). The coating acts like insulation and allows messages to travel quickly without any loss of transmission. Currently two theories describe the production and release of myelin.

One theory, supported by neurophysiologist Carla Hannaford (1995), says that myelin is added to the axon with use. In other words, as the neuron is called upon to fire, a coating of myelin is put down. If the neuron is part of a network of neurons fired often, the axon will be heavily myelinated. So, like the path in the woods that is constantly walked upon, the neuronal path becomes smoother and faster.

Myelin acts as insulation on the axon, making messages move more quickly.

Other researchers, like Jane Healy (1994), theorize that the myelination of neurons is a developmental process that begins at birth. According to this theory, the brain releases myelin in stages, beginning with the

There are two theories on how the process of myelination takes place.

lower brain areas. The final area of the brain to be myelinated is in the prefrontal cortex behind the forehead. This is where decision making, planning, and many higher-order thinking skills take place. This area is also associated with short-term memory.

What are the implications of these two theories? Could both be correct? In my study of the brain, I have read about both ideas and observed how the researchers have swung both ways on this pendulum. Let's look at some facts.

The development of the brain from birth through the end of adolescence parallels the child development stages identified by Jean Piaget. The researchers who believe in the developmental release of myelin state that the stages of myelin release coincide with Piaget's developmental stages (see figure 1.4). Piaget identifies four developmental stages:

• Sensorimotor stage (birth–2 years)—At this stage the child interacts physically with the environment. She builds a set of ideas about reality and how it works.

• Pre-operational stage (ages 2–7)—At this stage the child is not yet able to think abstractly. She needs concrete physical situations.

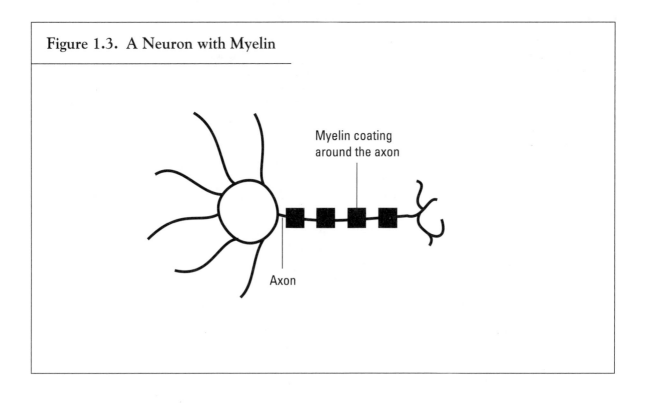

Figure 1.3. A Neuron with Myelin

Myelin coating around the axon

Axon

• Concrete operations (ages 7–11)—At this stage the child has accumulated enough experiences to begin to conceptualize and to do some abstract problem solving, though the child still learns best by doing.

• Formal operations (ages 11–15)—At this stage the child's thought processes are beginning to be like those of an adult.

Figure 1.4 suggests substantial support for this theory. Jane Healy (1994) states that the largest release of myelin may occur in the adolescent years. Once this dose is released, children have an easier time making decisions, planning for the future, and working out problems.

Although Piaget suggests that this stage occurs between the ages of 11 and 15, current research suggests that this stage varies with the individual. After spending some time teaching at the high school level, I have observed that many students appear to reach this final stage during their sophomore year, though some don't quite make it until senior year or afterward. Only 50 percent of the adult population reach this stage at all (Jensen, 1998).

Short-term memory does not reach capacity until approximately the age of 15. The capacity of short-term memory in a fully developed brain is seven chunks of information. At age 3, space exists for only one chunk. With the discovery by researchers like LeDoux (1996) that short-term memory is held in the frontal lobes, the last area myelinated, it makes sense that the frontal lobe's incomplete development due to the lack of myelin would influence short-term memory.

Many students today have difficulty with higher-order thinking skills. Although children of every age have some ability to synthesize, abstract, and evaluate, some children have more difficulty than others. Realizing that this difficulty may be due to the lack of myelin or its delayed release could

Figure 1.4 indicates some support for the theory of developmental release of myelin.

Formal thinking operations and the last release of myelin may not occur until late adolescence.

Higher-order thinking skills and myelin release may be related.

Delayed release of myelin could affect abilities to learn.

Figure 1.4. Piaget's Stages and the Stages of Brain Development

Piaget's Four Stages of Child Development	Four Stages of Myelin Release & Brain Growth
Sensorimotor (birth–2 years)	Large Motor System and Visual System
Pre-operational (ages 2–7)	Language Acquisition
Concrete Operations (ages 7–11)	Manipulate Thoughts and Ideas
Formal Operations (ages 11–15)	Higher-Order Thinking

lessen both children's frustration and that of the adults trying to help them.

Smooth transfer of information from neuron to neuron is greatly dependent on myelin. My two 4-year-old neighbors are a joy to watch. Their development and interests are very different. Joey loves to do acrobatics. He can do cartwheels better than I ever dreamed of doing them. He can almost do flips, and he loves any type of physical adventure. On the other hand, Mark is not very agile. He has difficulty doing somersaults. Instead of concentrating on the physical world, Mark is trying to read. He is constantly bugging his mother to tell him what written words say. Mark knows the alphabet and can spell some words.

Both boys are normal preschoolers. They are simply developing differently. Carla Hannaford (1995) believes that children benefit when neuronal connections are made through body movement. These connections will help them develop the neuronal systems for reading when they are ready. These boys obviously have different interests, which may have been inspired by their environments. Joey's sisters are acrobats, and perhaps he received recognition for mimicking their behavior. Because Mark is the older sibling in his family, he may be exhibiting behavior that he believes will win his parents' approval. Whatever the reasons, the firing of neurons is causing the learning.

The developmental differences among children are great. Whether these differences are caused by heredity or by the environment is a debate that continues. Whether myelin is released in stages or through use of the neurons, children still exhibit differences.

Myelin is a factor in brain growth and learning. I believe that both theories may be correct. It makes sense that as the brain continually uses its networks of neurons, transmission of information is swifter. It also makes sense that as their brains develop, children undergo vast changes.

Neuron Signals

Cartoonists often draw a lightbulb above the head to portray a character with an idea. This portrayal actually contains some element of truth. The brain has enough electrical power to light a 25-watt bulb. As mentioned previously, the process of neurons communicating is electro-chemical. The electrical part takes place within the neuron.

All matter has an electrical property. The electrical charges, called *ions*, are either positive or negative. The ions in the brain are sodium, potassium (each with one positive charge), calcium (with two positive charges), and chloride (with one negative charge). Some negatively charged protein molecules are also present. Neurons are surrounded by a

Developmental stages vary among children.

Learning is affected by environment.

The brain has enough electrical energy to light a 25-watt bulb.

Neurons are surrounded by a cell membrane that allows some ions to pass through.

cell membrane that may allow some ions to pass through and that block others. The openings in the cell membrane are called *channels*. While some channels remain open, others open only in response to chemical stimulation.

Resting Potential

When a neuron is not sending a signal, the area inside the neuron has more negatively charged ions, and the area outside has more positively charged ions. This is called its *resting potential* (see figure 1.5). At this level potassium ions pass through channels easily, but chloride and sodium ions have very few channels to flow through, and protein ions have none. All of the ions want to move across the membrane, but because only the positively charged potassium does so readily, the outside of the neuron is positive and the inside is negative. This balance keeps the neuron at rest. During this time the electrical charge inside the neuron can be measured at about negative 70 millivolts and the outside at positive 70 millivolts (Dowling, 1998).

The electrical charge inside a resting neuron is −70 millivolts. The electrical charge outside is +70.

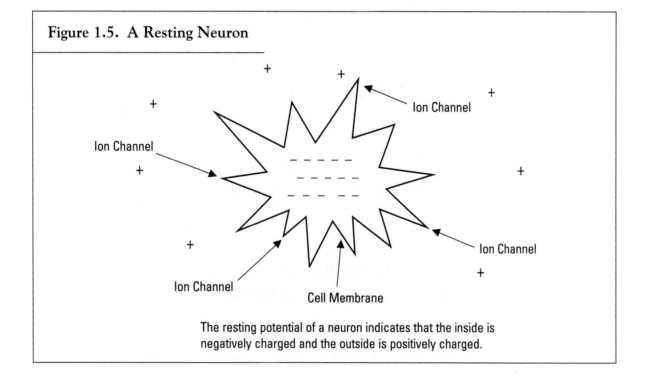

Figure 1.5. A Resting Neuron

Ion Channel

Ion Channel

Ion Channel

Ion Channel

Cell Membrane

The resting potential of a neuron indicates that the inside is negatively charged and the outside is positively charged.

Action Potential

When a chemical stimulus causes the opening of sodium channels, positively charged sodium ions rush into the negatively charged neuron, and the neuron becomes more positive (see figure 1.6). This state, called *action potential*, depolarizes the neuron. The millivolts within it increase, and at a voltage of about negative 55 millivolts the neuron fires. This firing is always of a fixed size. In other words, it is an all-or-nothing situation. This change in voltage causes an electrical energy output that sends the charge down the axon, across the synapse, and to the dendrites of the receiving neuron. Thus, a message is sent. When the potassium channels open again, potassium rushes out of the cell and the neuron goes back to resting potential.

Figure 1.6. An Active Neuron

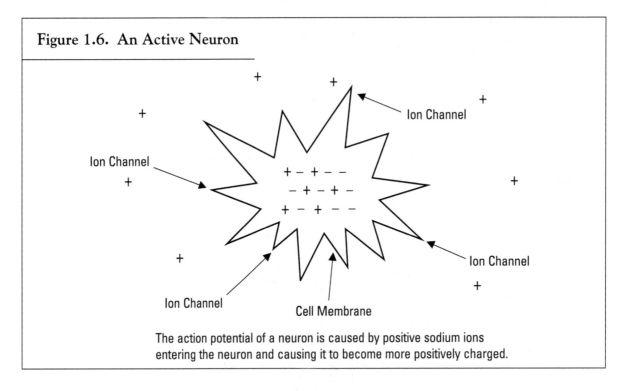

The action potential of a neuron is caused by positive sodium ions entering the neuron and causing it to become more positively charged.

Rats, Cats, Children, and Adults: How Do Their Dendrites Grow?

The brain's ability to grow and change is called *plasticity*. Neuronal activity, or the lack of it, causes these changes. The change process prompts questions such as these: How do we know it is happening? Where is the proof? Can it happen to anyone? Am I too old for brain growth? In other words, can you teach an old dog new tricks? The answers to these questions lie in years of research by some impressive neuroscientists. Let's examine the evidence.

Marian Diamond (1988) of the University of California at Berkeley has been studying the brain development of rats for more than 40 years, with impressive results. She and her colleagues and students conduct experiments in which they place rats in enriched environments. They use control groups to check for accuracy. In one of her tests, she placed a single rat in a regular rat cage—no fun toys for this one. The rat was given food and water as a normal lab rat would be. A larger cage housed one rat with toys. This rat also was tended to in a normal fashion. Then there was the fancy group—12 rats in a large cage containing rat toys, such as wheels to run on, trails to follow, and blocks to climb. The last cage housed 12 rats with no toys. Diamond called the cages with toys *enriched* environments and those without toys *impoverished*. The control group for this study consisted of three rats in a small cage with no toys.

The results of this study are exciting. Rats in the enriched environments (those with toys) had more dendritic connections than the rats in the impoverished environments; the dendritic branches were thicker as well (see figure 1.7). The study also showed that the control group with three rats learned more than either the rat left alone in the impoverished environment or the rat left alone in the enriched environment. Diamond concluded that the rats learned more by living together and even more by living together in an enriched environment.

Studies like this led to even more studies using rats. The rat brain is very similar in structure to the human brain, but because it has fewer "wrinkles," it is easier to measure.

William Greenough of the University of Illinois discovered that rats in enriched environments had 25 percent more connections between neurons and performed much better in tests (Kotulak, 1996). He believes that synapses can be formed in seconds! (More dendrites create more synapses.) Researchers have found proof of changes in the brains of rats after only four days. In four days dendritic growth as a result of enrichment can occur, and in four more days dendritic death can occur as a result of lack of stimulation (Hooper & Teresi, 1986).

As an educator, I have a favorite rat story. In a 1985 study, Diamond placed baby rats and mature rats in the same enriched cage. She wanted to know if both the young rats and the older rats would grow more dendrites. The surprise came when the older rats refused to let the young rats play with the toys. The mature rats took over the cage and did not allow the baby rats to play. The result was that only the mature rats grew dendrites.

You *can* teach an old dog new tricks.

Enriched environments encourage dendritic growth.

Studies of rats suggest that learning is a social experience.

Even in an enriched environment, the individual must be active in order to stimulate the growth of dendrites.

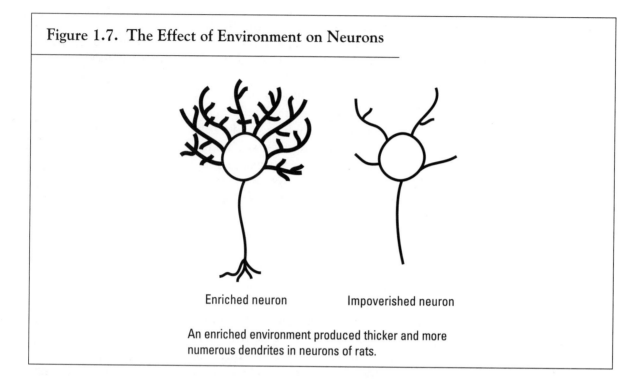

Figure 1.7. The Effect of Environment on Neurons

Enriched neuron   Impoverished neuron

An enriched environment produced thicker and more numerous dendrites in neurons of rats.

Why do I like this story? When I walk past classrooms with high-tech equipment such as computers, I like to watch what is happening. Often I see the teacher (the old rat) sitting at the computer showing the students how to do something. The students are sitting and watching. Who's growing dendrites here—the old rat or the babies?

We can conclude from Diamond's study that it isn't enough for students to be in an enriched environment. They need to help create that environment and be active in it.

Touch may add to the life span of rats.

Another rat study really intrigued me. During a visit to Japan to observe Japanese researchers' work with rats, Diamond learned that the Japanese rats were living to be 900 days old, which equals about 90 years for humans. Diamond's rats had been living only about 700 days, which is an expected life span for a laboratory rat. Intrigued, Diamond looked for differences between the two groups of rats. The food, temperature, and cages seemed to be similar for both groups. However, she did notice one difference. In Japan the lab assistants held the rats while the cages were being cleaned. In Diamond's studies, the rats were simply put into another cage. She concluded that this touching and holding may have increased the rats' life span. In addition, because the rats were not put into a "strange" cage while their own was being cleaned, they may have felt less

Stress can prevent brain growth and shorten life span.

stress. After Diamond returned to the United States, she instructed her lab assistants to hold the rats. The rats began living beyond their 700 days and had more dendritic connections than rats that were not held (Wolfe, 1996). We can conclude that gentle care can add to life span and contribute to brain growth.

Researchers have also conducted several studies with kittens. One study involved taking identical twin kittens at a critical time in their visual development and placing them in a large, circular container painted with black and white vertical stripes. These lines were the kittens' only visual stimulation. A balance beam with a basket on each end revolved in the center of the container. Each twin was placed in a basket. One of the baskets had holes for the kitten's legs, while the other did not. The kitten whose legs could go through the basket and touch the ground began walking around the container. His twin brother had a free ride. What the researchers discovered is truly amazing. The kitten who did the work and interacted with his environment developed great vision for vertical lines. The kitten who did not work could not see vertical lines at all (Healy, 1990). We can conclude that experiences cause brain growth, but one must actively participate in the experiences for growth to take place.

> Active participation in experiences encourages brain growth.

Now that we've talked about rats and cats, let's look at children and adults. After studying the results of such researchers as Greenough, Craig Ramey of the University of Alabama designed a study with children from an inner-city, impoverished environment (Kotulak, 1996). He took a group of children as young as 6 weeks old and exposed them to an enriched environment with playmates, good nutrition, and opportunities for learning and playing. Ramey followed this group and a control group for 12 years. Using intelligence tests and brain-imaging techniques, he found a significant difference in the way in which the children's brains had developed. The enriched children had significantly higher IQs, and brain imaging revealed that their brains were using energy much more efficiently, according to the scans. We can conclude that the brain is sensitive to its early environment and that enrichment can make a difference.

> Learning, playing, good nutrition, and playmates all contribute to an enriched environment for everyone.

> The brain is sensitive to its early environment.

What can we do about growing dendrites? Researchers are addressing this question with a group of nuns in Mankato, Minnesota, who are participating in a study to examine the effects of remaining mentally and physically active in their work and daily lives. These women have lived well beyond the average life span, and researchers attribute their longevity to their active lifestyle. They constantly stimulate and challenge their brains (Golden, 1994).

> No matter how old you are, stimulating and challenging your brain will add to your life span and foster brain growth.

Studies have compared the IQs of people in nursing homes with the IQs of those waiting to be admitted. People in the nursing homes have significantly lower IQs than those awaiting admission. In many cases, IQs go down measurably after just six months in a nursing home (Hooper & Teresi, 1986). Enriched environments can make a huge difference for everyone.

What Can We Learn from These Studies?

We can draw a number of conclusions from these studies. First, from the rat studies, a *social* environment is a form of enrichment. Rats do better when they interact with other rats and solve problems together. Humans are social creatures, and learning is a social activity. Gentle *care* was also a factor for the rats. We must take care when we work with others to help them in their quest for learning. Second, the studies with cats indicate that we need to *interact* with our environment. That means that both kittens must be able to walk around the container. We need to work together and all take part in the learning. Third, the studies of children tell us that the brain is very sensitive to its early environment, and enrichment affects its growth. Fourth, the study involving nuns indicates that brain stimulation at any age is important and helpful. Our lives must include some *challenges*. And the children, the rats, the cats, and the nuns tell us that *play* is important for learning.

Social interaction, care, challenge, and play are important for growing those dendrites. Whether it be in the classroom, in the home, at work, or in the community, all of these factors influence how much we learn.

Learning is a social activity: We learn better when we work together.

2

Chicken Soup for the Brain:
The Effects of Brain Chemicals

I am trying to catch up on my journal reading late one evening when the phone rings, and I am torn away from an article on learning styles and the brain.

At first, I do not recognize the woman's voice. She says, "Hey, there. Do you have your nose buried in some book?"

I immediately try to defend myself: "No, I'm relaxing with a magazine."

"I just bet it's some educational article you're reading and not Martha Stewart."

Hearing the voice again, I realize I am talking to an old college friend, Maggie. "Why aren't you at some wild party?" I reply, trying to give her a taste of her own medicine. Maggie and I had different interests in college; she was a party person, while I took my studies very seriously. However, we enjoyed teasing each other about our interests and had found a bond in that.

"I stayed home from the parties tonight because I need to talk to you about my daughter," she says with some emotion.

I begin to search my mind for her daughter's name, and suddenly "Michelle" pops up. "How is Michelle doing?"

"We're having some problems, and I am hoping with your brain research knowledge you can tell me what to do," Maggie replies.

"I'm not a doctor, but you know I'll help in whatever way I can."

She begins to blurt out a story that is shocking but like many others reported in the newspapers. "Michelle was at a party a few months ago. You know, one of those college parties with plenty of drinking. A friend of hers drank way too much. Actually, I think he was more than a friend, and Mar, he died! Alcoholic poisoning. Michelle just hasn't been the same since."

Just as chicken soup makes your body feel better, chemicals produced in your brain make it feel better.

These chemicals affect memories, learning, and relationships.

The thoughts we have, the food we eat, and the drugs we take all have an effect on these chemicals.

At least 60 chemicals have been identified, and more will likely be identified.

"Oh my gosh! The poor thing. How is she doing?"

"That's just it. She's a mess. She can't study. She can't think. The doctors want to put her on some drug."

"Well, that sounds reasonable. What do they want to put her on?"

"I'm really embarrassed about this. It's one of those antidepressants. That's why I'm calling you. What is this stuff going to do to her? Happy pills aren't going to make her better! I think she just needs to talk to a shrink and get it over with. What do you think?"

I take a deep breath and search my brain for the right things to say to my overwrought friend. Like most parents, she wants to help her daughter, and she doesn't want the world to think that anything is wrong with her. I gather my thoughts and begin: "Those drugs are similar to the chicken soup your mom used to make so you would feel better when you were ill. Drugs, such as antidepressants, that affect the chemicals in your brain can help your brain deal with problems. They aren't 'happy pills.' In fact, from what we know about them, they won't make you feel better unless you really need them."

Your brain runs on chemicals. Scientists have identified at least 60 different brain chemicals and are certain that there are more (Sylwester, 1997a). Sometimes these chemicals are referred to as *peptides* or *neurohormones*, but most researchers call them *neurotransmitters*. These neurotransmitters are affected by our actions and our thoughts. We can also affect them by the foods we eat. We cannot underestimate their value nor their effect upon us.

The chemicals that run the brain are called neurotransmitters.

How Neurotransmitters Work

Neurotransmitters are chemicals that carry information from one neuron to another.

Neurotransmitters are chemicals that carry information from one neuron to another. Remember that the transmission *within* the neuron is electrical, and the transmission *between* neurons is chemical. The electrical impulse causes small vesicles in the axon of the neuron to release the neurotransmitters, which then swim across the synapse (the small space between neurons) and attach themselves to the dendrites of the receiving neuron (see figure 2.1).

Neurotransmitters act like keys. Each one has its own special type of receptor and will not fit into others.

This whole effect has been compared to a lock and key. Like keys, the neurotransmitters fit into small receptor sites on the dendrites. Each neurotransmitter has its own special type of receptor and will not fit into others. It is important to note that some neurotransmitters are *excitatory*, that is, they cause the next neuron to fire; others are *inhibitory* and stop the neuron from firing. Neurons can receive both excitatory and inhibitory messages simultaneously. Then it becomes a question of power. If the

Figure 2.1. The Electrical and Chemical Activity of Neurons

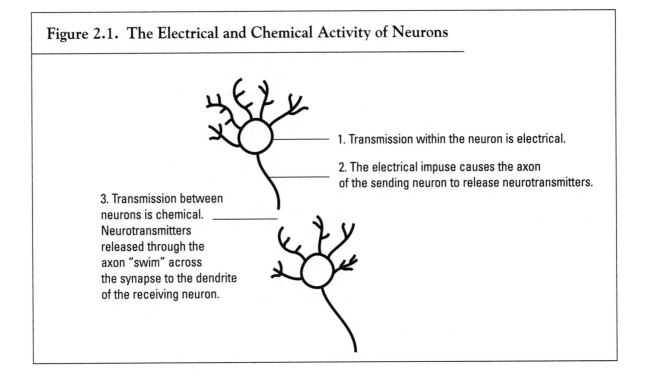

1. Transmission within the neuron is electrical.

2. The electrical impuse causes the axon of the sending neuron to release neurotransmitters.

3. Transmission between neurons is chemical. Neurotransmitters released through the axon "swim" across the synapse to the dendrite of the receiving neuron.

excitatory neurotransmitter has more receptors than the inhibitory neurotransmitter, the neuron will fire (Restak, 1995).

When a neuron receives a message repeatedly, the effect is called *strengthening the synapse*. Receptor sites increase in number, giving the chemical message more areas of attachment. Efficiency increases, and transmission becomes faster and easier. This is a desirable occurrence when it comes to learning important information, and practice leads the brain to easily process that information. But it becomes undesirable in situations such as the use of drugs. When a person uses addictive drugs, the brain also forms receptor sites for the drug molecules. The abundance of these receptor sites causes some of the physical difficulty in withdrawing from the drug. After a time, if the receptor sites are not used (following withdrawal and drug rehabilitation), the brain prunes or replaces them.

As the brain makes and strengthens connections, outside factors can easily influence it. These factors may include addictive substances, as well as something as simple as the food you eat.

It's the day of the big test. Sherry awakens early to study. She reviews her notes as she paces in her room. In the shower she continues to

When a neuron receives a message repeatedly, the connection is strengthened.

The brain is easily influenced by outside factors.

Are we what we eat?

practice the lists of information she must recall for this final exam. As she dresses, she stares at her textbook and the tables she must memorize. Her mother calls her for breakfast.

Sherry carries her notes with her to the table. She realizes that she is not very hungry, so she glances over the offerings until she sees the cinnamon rolls, her favorite. She snatches two rolls and dashes out the door. Sherry hopes she can study with her friends before the exam.

A similar scenario is taking place at Sean's house. He has been studying for an hour before breakfast. Like Sherry, Sean takes his notes to the breakfast table and continues to review. He, however, decides to eat some scrambled eggs, toast, and a glass of milk. Finishing quickly, Sean grabs his materials and heads to school for further study.

Neurotransmitters affect how we feel and how we act.

About 30 minutes later, both students are bent over their tests, regurgitating material they were told to study. Sean is alert and doing well. Sherry is starting to feel sleepy. She searches her brain for information she knows is there, but she has trouble finding it. Her head is in her hands; she yawns repeatedly.

Are We What We Eat?

What is the difference between these two students and their ability to take the test? It may very well be the foods they have eaten. Many researchers now suggest that we are what we eat. The food we eat may affect the neurotransmitters being released in our brain, and, therefore, affect whether our neurons are firing. Sherry ate food high in carbohydrates, which are suspected of causing the release of the inhibitory neurotransmitter *serotonin*. This inhibitor causes sleepiness. Therefore, she is not as alert as she needs to be for the exam. Sean, on the other hand, ate foods high in protein. Protein keeps the serotonin from being released and helps with alertness and focus (Wurtman & Suffes, 1996).

Eating protein can inhibit some of the neurotransmitters that cause sleepiness.

Those cinnamon rolls that Sherry ate probably also contain a great deal of fat. Fat digests more slowly than other foods. Therefore, a great deal of her blood supply had to be in her digestive tract helping with the digestive process. She needed that blood to go to her brain to help her make the connections she needed. This also could have affected her performance.

Ready. Aim. Fire?

We don't want all of our neurons to fire at once!

What would happen if all of our neurons fired at once? We would probably go crazy as our brain experienced every piece of information being received as well as information already stored. The combination of the neurotransmitters both causing and preventing the firing action is what helps the messages travel to the appropriate areas of the brain and what helps us make sense of the world. This combination helps us to both "pay attention to" and "block out" stimuli.

A good analogy for this phenomenon is a theater marquee—the kind with lots of lightbulbs and changing patterns that form different words. If too many of the bulbs are lit, the message is unclear. If none of the bulbs is lit, the message doesn't exist. However, if the correct combination of bulbs is on, the message is clear (see figure 2.2). In this same way, if the correct pattern of neurons is firing and the others are not, information is readily available to the brain, and it makes sense. The brain is always searching for meaning and patterns (Wolfe, 1996).

The formation and action of neurotransmitters involves the following steps:

> When the correct neurons fire, a message is sent.

1. Enzymes acting upon specific substances within the cell produce a chemical—the neurotransmitter—inside the neuron.

2. These newly synthesized neurotransmitters are stored in vesicles.

3. Activation of the neuron releases the neurotransmitters.

4. The released neurotransmitter molecules cross the synapse and bind with the receiving neuron at their special receptor sites.

> Neurotransmitters flow from the axon terminal of the sending neuron to the receptor sites on the dendrite of the receiving neuron.

Figure 2.2. A Clear Message

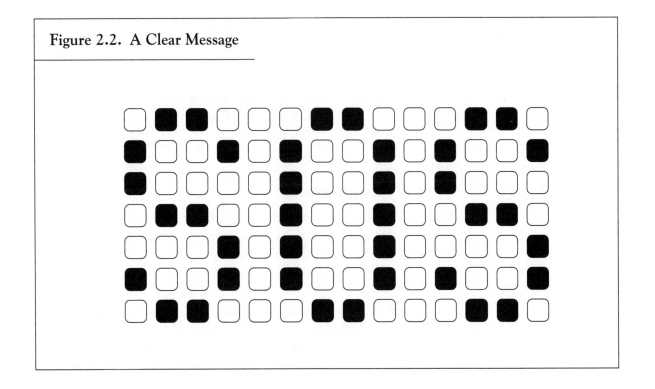

5. The receiving neuron is either activated by the message, causing the neuron to fire, or it is inhibited by it, preventing it from firing.

6. The released neurotransmitter molecules are destroyed by enzymes in the synapse or are taken back by the sending neuron. This is called "re-uptake." All molecules are available for reuptake.

Figure 2.3 illustrates part of the process. As stated earlier, the receptors prepare for only a specific chemical, and they accept no others.

Figure 2.3. Storage and Movement of Neurotransmitters

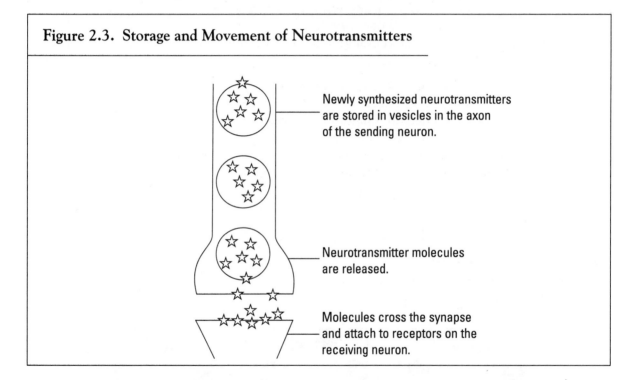

Newly synthesized neurotransmitters are stored in vesicles in the axon of the sending neuron.

Neurotransmitter molecules are released.

Molecules cross the synapse and attach to receptors on the receiving neuron.

Types of Neurotransmitters

Now let's look at some specific neurotransmitters and how they affect the brain. Neurotransmitters are usually divided into three groups: *amino acids, monoamines,* and *peptides* (see figure 2.4.)

Amino Acids

The two amino acid neurotransmitters that we need to be aware of are *glutamate* and GABA (gamma-aminobutyric acid). Glutamate always carries an excitatory message and is, in fact, the most prevalent excitatory neurotransmitter in the brain. GABA always carries an inhibitory message. It is actually made from glutamate with one extra enzyme. GABA exists in the areas of the brain dealing with emotions and thinking. Glutamate and GABA appear in most information-processing transmissions as one activates certain neurons and the other quiets those that are not needed for the message.

Some neurotransmitters are excitatory, and others are inhibitory.

Figure 2.4. Classes of Neurotransmitters

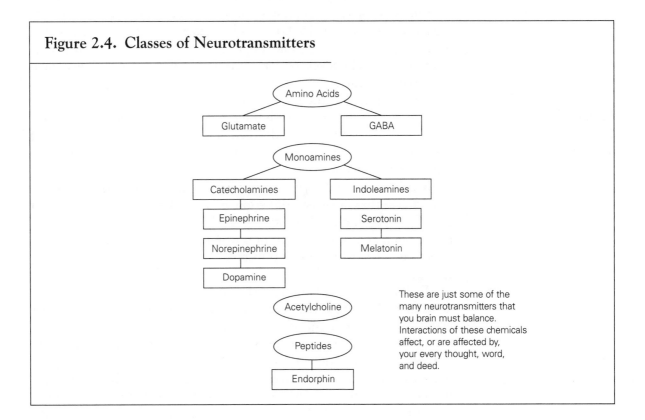

These are just some of the many neurotransmitters that you brain must balance. Interactions of these chemicals affect, or are affected by, your every thought, word, and deed.

Monoamines

Monoamines are divided into two classes: *catecholamines* and *indoleamines*. The catecholamines include the neurotransmitters *epinephrine*, *norepinephrine*, and *dopamine*, and the indoleamines include *serotonin* and *melatonin*.

Epinephrine is another name for adrenaline. It is released by the adrenal glands, which are located above the kidneys. Epinephrine gets your body moving in situations that call for instant action—such as those that involve fear or danger (Calvin & Ojemann, 1994). Just as *epinephrine* gets your body's attention, *norepinephrine* gets your brain's attention. This excitatory neurotransmitter makes your brain alert.

Epinephrine gets the body moving in situations that require instant action, such as those involving fear or danger.

Dopamine is one of the chemicals that helps information flow to higher levels in the brain.

The main function of *dopamine* is to control physical movement. This inhibitory neurotransmitter is important for executing smooth movement. It is associated with Parkinson's disease, characterized by constant muscle movement. The lack of dopamine causes these symptoms. In some cases, a drug called L-dopa helps the dopamine-producing neurons continue to manufacture the neurotransmitter (Calvin & Ojemann, 1994). Dopamine is also related to the regulation of the flow of information into higher levels of the brain. Low levels of dopamine may affect working memory (see chapter 4), and high levels have been associated with schizophrenia. The levels of dopamine appear to decline with age; men tend to have greater losses than women. Dopamine has euphoric effects that are magnified by the intake of alcohol (Kotulak, 1996).

Serotonin is sometimes called the "feel good" neurotransmitter.

The indoleamine *serotonin* is sometimes called the "feel good" neurotransmitter. Researchers have devoted much time and money to studying this chemical—with important results. This neurotransmitter has a significant effect on our lives.

Serotonin aids in smooth transmission of messages in the brain and the body.

Researchers first discovered serotonin in the digestive system, where they found that it assists digestion and regulates the movement of smooth, large muscles (Sylwester, 1995). Later scientists traced serotonin to the brain and began to question whether serotonin might also have something to do with smooth transmission of messages within the brain. It does.

To illustrate how serotonin works, I pose the following problem to students in my brain research classes: How can I throw a beach ball all the way across a room in one attempt? Because I don't have much strength and the ball doesn't have enough weight to remain aloft across the entire distance, I will need help. I decide that another participant can help me by picking up the ball and carrying it over to my friend at the other end of the room. This solution works well. I throw the ball. Participant A carries it over to participant B. Mission accomplished! I can send as many balls over to B as I want, because A is there to help me. However, what if I decide I don't want A to leave me, and I hold on to her hand? I begin to have trouble getting the ball across the room again. Yet, I really don't want A to leave. No matter how hard I try, I can't get that ball across the room.

Sometimes serotonin or other neurotransmitters are taken back by their sending neuron.

Well, let's call the ball a message. I am Neuron 1 sending the message. Neuron 2 is the person receiving the message. My helper is the neurotransmitter serotonin. Its job is to help deliver messages throughout the brain. Usually, it can be found in the spaces between neurons. Sometimes, however, after serotonin delivers to the receiving neuron, it is sucked back up by the sending neuron (reuptake). Therefore, it is no longer available in the synapse to send messages. Recall from the description of the action of neurotransmitters that, after activation, they are either destroyed or taken back by the sending neuron. This reuptake can cause problems with future transmissions.

Serotonin is produced in the lower brain regions just above the spinal cord. However, the neurons that produce serotonin have very long axons that extend throughout the brain. Serotonin may very well be a part of every message sent. If serotonin is left to circulate, it can stimulate neurons for a longer period. This may allow for better transmission and stronger messages (Lemonick, 1997).

My study of the research on serotonin has led me to appreciate its power. A lack of serotonin appears to keep many individuals "trapped" in the emotional areas of their brains. This causes low self-esteem and depression.

Scientists have developed many antidepressant drugs to help control serotonin levels. My friend Maggie was concerned about the label "antidepressant" and how such a drug would affect her daughter. The idea that these are "happy pills" is mistaken. The antidepressant drugs that are labeled SSRIs are specific serotonin reuptake inhibitors. This means that they inhibit the reuptake of serotonin at certain receptor sites. They do not produce more serotonin. They simply allow more serotonin to flow freely throughout certain areas of the brain. They act like corks and block the reuptake channels. Typically this allows information to flow more freely and makes the individual feel better. SSRIs work in subtle ways and take several weeks to be fully effective.

The indoleamine *melatonin* is a neurotransmitter that has received much attention in the 1990s. Advertisements claim that regular doses of melatonin can make one look younger, feel better, and sleep well. Researchers are proving most of this information false. However, melatonin *is* related to sleep. It is a chemical released from the pineal gland, which is located in the forebrain. Upon its release, drowsiness occurs. Our biological clock activates melatonin. Many travelers have used melatonin supplements to overcome jet lag (Wolfe, 1996).

Acetylcholine is in a class by itself. Although it is not truly a monoamine, it is often associated with that category of neurotransmitters. Produced in a subcortical area above the brain stem and found throughout the brain, acetylcholine operates voluntary and involuntary muscle movements (Sylwester, 1995). One interesting finding is that it appears in the brain in vast amounts while we are sleeping. It is the chemical that causes many of our dreams, and it is directly related to memory. Recent research suggests that one purpose of sleep is to allow the brain to practice what it has learned during the day. The presence of acetylcholine during this time indicates the importance of the chemical in cementing learning into long-term memory. Acetylcholine is formed in

---

Serotonin may well be a part of every message sent.

A lack of serotonin may result in low self-esteem and depression.

Melatonin is a chemical related to the wake/sleep cycle.

Acetylcholine is in a class by itself.

Acetylcholine is an important neurotransmitter related to memory. It is the chemical responsible for many dreams.

the brain with the help of certain fats in our diets (Hobson, 1994). Fat-free diets, therefore, could be detrimental to learning experiences. A shortage of acetylcholine has been linked to a poor ability to concentrate, forgetfulness, and disturbing sleep patterns.

Peptides

Many chemicals come under this category. One, however, stands out: *endorphin*. In 1973 two scientists discovered the opiate receptors in the brain. The finding led to the discovery that the brain makes its own natural morphine. The name of this substance, called *endogenous morphine*, was later shortened to *endorphin* (Pert, 1997). Endorphins are the body's natural anesthetics, and they are powerful pain killers. Women in childbirth produce 10 times the normal amounts of endorphins (Wolfe, 1996). You may have heard the term "runner's high." This term emerged because running and other activities cause the release of a great deal of endorphin, and an abundance of it causes a feeling of euphoria.

In 1977 researchers conducted a study to determine how the level of endorphin affects a person's enjoyment of music. Because many people describe their positive experiences with music as causing pleasurable sensations, scientists gave the participants in the study endorphin blockers. When the release of the endorphins was blocked and the participants listened to their favorite music, an odd thing happened. They did not enjoy the music as much as usual. When the blocker had worn off, they once again derived pleasure from listening to the music (Hooper & Teresi, 1986). Endorphins have, therefore, been labeled as part of the reward system of the brain (Jourdain, 1997).

The final brain chemical to consider is called *cortisol*. Like the monoamine epinephrine, this peptide is released by the adrenal glands, located above the kidneys. Once released, it travels to the brain to do much of its work.

Many scientists consider cortisol to be a hormone. Although it has some positive effects at low levels, it can be very toxic to the brain and body at high levels. Cortisol is a stress-related substance. The hypothalamus calls for its release when the brain feels threatened. Cortisol, along with adrenaline, aids in the "flight or fight" response (LeDoux, 1996).

Our stress responses cannot differentiate between emotional and physical danger. Therefore, cortisol may be released during slight emotional upheavals. Chronic stress causes it to be released at high levels that can damage certain brain structures, interrupt transmission of messages from neuron to neuron, and cause immune, circulatory, and digestive problems.

Endorphin is the body's natural pain killer.

An abundance of endorphin may create a feeling of euphoria.

Cortisol is a chemical released when we are under stress; at high levels it can be dangerous.

Stress responses cannot differentiate between emotional and physical danger.

Behavior and Neurotransmitters

It is important to understand the powerful influence that serotonin, dopamine, endorphin, and norepinephrine have on behavior. High levels of norepinephrine can cause aggression. The other three neurotransmitters can keep this behavior somewhat under control.

Can levels of serotonin, dopamine, and endorphin be affected by means of a pathway that does not include invading the brain? The answer is yes. The brain may release serotonin, dopamine, and endorphin as the result of exercise, an affirming touch or smile, or a meaningful relationship (Glenn, 1990). In addition, the single most dynamic influence on the brain's chemistry may be positive feedback. Positive feedback, which comes in many different forms, is essential for the development of a good self-concept and healthy self-esteem (Sylwester, 1997c). Serotonin, dopamine, and endorphin make the body feel good, aid the immune system, and help in transmitting messages easily and quickly. To a certain extent we can control our own levels of these natural drugs, and we can affect others' levels.

Can we do this in a classroom? Yes. It can be as easy as allowing students to stand up and stretch, playing Simon Says, or doing the hokey-pokey. Each of these is a form of exercise and will raise respiration and heart rates enough for the body to begin releasing these chemicals. Shaking students' hands provides those affirming touches. A pat on the back, some high-fives, or an innocent touch on the shoulder are other ways of releasing more chemicals. Providing students the opportunity to be a part of a significant relationship can be a bit harder, because time limits the development of a one-on-one relationship with every student. Teaming, however, can help students feel they are a part of something, cared for, and appreciated. The brain will then release the "feel good" chemicals such as endorphin and dopamine (Jensen, 1998). Music is another possible trigger for the release of positive chemicals. Researchers are studying the positive effects of music in the classroom and at home. If you listen to music you like, your brain will release these neurotransmitters. Singing may do the same thing. No one should be forced to sing, but if the singing is in a large group and everyone is comfortable, the result may be a room full of healthy and happy brains!

The Joy of Retirement?

Jim had finally decided to take that step. He had been teaching for 35 years, and he had to admit that he was tired. Coaching had taken so much time from his family that he couldn't remember a really great vacation. Jim's summers had always been spent coaching at basketball

> Behavior is influenced by serotonin, dopamine, endorphin, and norepinephrine.

> Positive feedback may be the single most powerful influence on the brain's chemistry.

> There are ways to influence the release of these chemicals.

> Teaming and movement may stimulate the brain to release the positive chemicals.

> Music and singing may encourage the brain's release of these chemicals.

Anyone may experience a neurotransmitter imbalance at varying times in life.

camps. The family needed the money; three sets of college expenses and all of those cars had really put a strain on the family's finances. The kids were graduated, married, and on their own now. So this really was the perfect time for retirement. After all, he and Mary were still young enough to enjoy life. As much as Jim loved teaching and coaching, physically it was really difficult to keep up with those kids—and those young coaches. Yes, it was time.

After he retired, a not-so-funny thing started happening around Jim's house. Jim just wasn't himself. He stayed in bed for a good part of the day. Mary would go out and play bridge with her friends, go to exercise class, and work in the garden. Jim didn't seem to have an interest in anything. Sometimes he wandered the house all night, and he rarely went out. Mary even caught Jim crying a few times when she was awakened by his nightly walks around the house.

Finally, Mary got Jim to go to the doctor. They were quite surprised when Jim's physician told him he was suffering from depression. The doctor prescribed an antidepressant, plenty of fresh air and exercise, and ordered Jim to find a hobby and a therapist.

Feeling good about ourselves is vital to a natural chemical balance.

It took about four weeks before Jim felt better. Mary nagged him until he started walking with her every day. Then he went to the YMCA and began volunteering his time with the kids in the gym. Soon he began to feel good again. Retirement was okay. He didn't need to be at school and working to feel good about himself.

Job satisfaction may help in the natural production of positive chemicals.

What happened to Jim could happen to anyone. It's a very common occurrence these days. Jim's brain chemistry changed when he quit working. His brain just wasn't producing an abundance of those feel-good neurotransmitters, especially serotonin, anymore. Jim had received many of those chemicals through his satisfaction with his work. He had received positive feedback from his students, his colleagues, and his superiors. Jim had thrown himself into his work for 35 years and did not have much of an outside life. When he retired, the chemicals quit flowing. As a result, he became clinically depressed and was left with some very negative emotions. Missing were the neurotransmitters necessary for the logical part of his brain to make decisions and plans.

Depression has been described as an imbalance in the brain's chemistry.

In Jim's case, the antidepressant took effect in four weeks and allowed him to have enough chemicals available to start doing things that then helped him avoid depression. He started receiving positive feedback as a result of the walks with his wife and his work at the gym. Over time, additional contacts will help him lead a happy life once again.

This scenario is common among retired and elderly people. The same thing can happen to children. In the case of my friend's daughter, a traumatic incident caused the chemical problem. Michelle was feeling guilty and responsible for her friend's death. His death also caused her to feel alone and afraid. Nothing in her life seemed positive anymore. The doctors prescribed medication to help her recover.

These examples are offered not to promote the use of antidepressants or other drugs to solve problems, but to show you how the brain and its chemicals can be easily affected. The good news is that science now sees these drugs as short-term therapy. Both Michelle and Jim will need to talk to a counselor or therapist to work through their problems. The antidepressants simply help raise their chemical levels so that they can deal with the problems.

Now that we have looked at some extreme cases, let's look at what could happen in a classroom under milder, yet similar, circumstances.

A Troubled Student?

Johnny transfers to your school from another neighborhood. In the old neighborhood, his friends considered Johnny to be very cool, and his teachers liked him. He didn't cause much trouble, he was a leader, and his grades were quite good. Compared with many of his former classmates, Johnny was an asset in the classroom.

Your school has a different sort of clientele. You teach in a rather affluent area. Most of your students are driven to get good grades, and they enjoy performing. Johnny doesn't shine in your school. Because his family is in a different economic situation from the majority, Johnny feels inferior to his new classmates.

Johnny begins to act out in class. He distracts other students and makes fun of the "eggheads." His grades begin to fall until he is receiving Ds. He seems to "forget" his materials and his homework. When you call home to talk to his parents, they are surprised and blame the situation on the new school.

What is going on in Johnny's mind? First, you can bet that Johnny's serotonin levels have dropped. He is no longer receiving positive feedback. He is no longer the leader of the pack. He is no longer a top student. Johnny is also under stress. He feels threatened by the new environment and by his fellow students. His cortisol levels are rising as he perceives himself in a "fight or flight" situation.

Because of the increased amount of cortisol, Johnny may not be thinking straight. If the cortisol is interrupting transmission between neurons, he probably feels even more threatened. The lower serotonin level may be affecting his norepinephrine level, causing him to be more aggressive. By acting out, he is looking for recognition from his peers. If he can't

Children, adults, and the elderly are all susceptible to chemical imbalances.

Classroom circumstances may affect the brain's chemistry in either a positive or a negative way.

An awareness of the brain's chemistry may help teachers affect the classroom environment.

When serotonin levels drop and cortisol levels rise, the result is the "fight or flight" response.

Even unhealthy self-esteem obtained from participating in behaviors such as gang activity can raise serotonin levels.

get that recognition in a positive way, he feels he has to get it any way he can. Remember, if he starts getting even negative attention, his brain may start producing more of the serotonin that it is probably craving. He has had many receptor sites for serotonin in the past, so his brain still seeks it.

This is definitely an at-risk child. He is at risk of dropping out of school at some point if he feels unsuccessful. He may be at risk for alcohol abuse or other drug habits that will make his brain believe that it is receiving the neurotransmitters it seeks. He may be at risk for joining a gang. In a gang he may feel important and may be a leader. That might help his brain produce those neurotransmitters, too.

The classroom may be the only place a student feels safe.

On the other hand, our classrooms may be the *only* place where some children feel safe and happy. They may be the only place where a student *isn't* under stress. There are probably lots of great chemicals being produced in our classrooms.

Making Chicken Soup in Your Classroom

How can you develop classroom environments that positively affect brain chemistry? *Begin by reducing stress as much as possible.* This is easier said than done. As a classroom teacher who sometimes fights for her own serotonin, I know that we are all under stress at times. The following suggestions may help:

Educators and parents can take many actions to provide a safe environment.

- Play calming music, such as selections from the Baroque era.
- Let students know that it's okay to make mistakes.
- Allow teamwork and social learning to help reduce tension.
- Celebrate learning, and let kids know that you understand they have feelings.
- Use movement like stretching or role-playing to add fun to learning.
- Provide an outlet for expression, such as journal writing.
- Give students some options and a feeling of some control over their lives.

Take care of yourself! Only then will you be able to affect your students.

- Take care of yourself! Your behavior one day is the best indicator of how your students will feel the next (Sylwester, 1997b). If you take care of yourself, you will be less stressed and more likely to provide a relaxed atmosphere for your students.

These suggestions can cause some dramatic, positive changes in the classroom.

I have to remind myself that my students' brains are still growing. As I think about how much time they spend with me, I realize what a large part of that growth I affect. I also remind myself that the brain is always looking for new information. It seeks stimulation. It is actually unnatural not to learn! Perhaps I can provide the environment that will help those brains to produce the appropriate chemicals for effective learning. Maybe this is just another kind of chicken soup that I can help make!

The brain desires a safe environment in which to seek new information and experiences.

3

Pieces and Parts:
The Anatomy of the Brain

It has been an extremely difficult week at school and at home. The class play had its final performance last night. I have been holding about seven rehearsals a week, and I am beat! I think I deserve a day off! This is not something I have ever done, but, by golly, other people do it. Why not me?

I ask my husband to call my principal and say that I am sick. (Okay, I'm a big chicken. I admit it!) He grudgingly does me the favor because he knows how tough the last month has been on me.

My husband leaves for work, and I roll over and try to fall asleep. After 15 minutes I am wide awake—and hungry! I dash to the kitchen and open the refrigerator door. Much to my dismay, there is no milk! You know those crazy people on the commercials who discover there is no milk? I become one of them. I have visions of making chocolate chip cookies and eating them warm and gooey straight from the oven. I can't do that without milk!

I call my sister-in-law to borrow some. Not home. I sit and ponder the entire situation. Can I possibly sneak into a grocery store and purchase milk without being seen? Do I take the chance? How about if I travel to a small town nearby? Yes! That's what I will do!

I throw on my sweats and my sunglasses. (Who cares that it's a cloudy day?) I drive 20 miles north of town to a supermarket. I walk into the store like a criminal, head down and collar up. I grab a basket for protection and head for the dairy aisle. I don't know where the milk is in this store, so I scan several aisles until I find it.

As I turn the corner to head for the checkout lane, I spot her. At the end of the next aisle is a blond woman with glasses. The assistant principal's wife! I do what any mature, responsible person would do. I turn around and run like an idiot! I go back to the dairy aisle and stand there

We are each vulnerable to the tricks our brains can play.

Our fears and our guilt may cause responses that we are not proud of.

The control that we pride ourselves on may be only an illusion!

shaking. My hands are clammy, my heart is beating like crazy, and I don't think I can take another breath. All I can think is that I am going to lose my job! After all of my years of dedication, I am going to lose my job because of chocolate chip cookies!

Wait a minute! Did she see me? Can I sneak out of here and get home before someone at the school finds out and calls me? That's it! I bend over my cart and steer toward the door. As I near the door, I push the cart backwards, run out to my car, jump behind the wheel, start the car, and head out of the parking lot. Checking the rearview mirror, I see the woman exiting the store. I slump down but keep an eye on her. I suddenly realize that this woman is much older than the assistant principal's wife and about 30 pounds heavier! It isn't her at all.

Do I dare turn back and get some milk? I think about my racing heart and my sweaty palms. No. I guess I'll skip the cookies today.

Why did I act like an idiot in that store? Why was my heart pounding and why were my palms sweating? Daniel Goleman (1995) would call my experience an "emotional hijacking," an experience that we all have at one time or another. The emotional parts of my brain were not allowing me to think with reason and logic. So I confused the woman in the store with my assistant principal's wife.

To understand situations such as this, we focus now on the bigger picture. It is time to look at how those 100 billion neurons and all of the glial cells that accompany them fit together in specific areas of the brain. Although the following sections label and discuss the functions of brain parts, keep in mind that to carry out intricate processes, the brain must work as a whole.

Fetal Development

At certain times in fetal brain development, neurons migrate to different areas of the brain. Some are earmarked as visual neurons, others as auditory, and still others become the various brain structures examined here. As the fetus grows and develops, different parts of the brain begin a maturation process. Some mature completely before birth, and others continue their growth well into life. The brain accounts for only about 2 to 3 percent of body weight; however, it uses 20 to 25 percent of the body's energy! Looking at it another way, that means that approximately every fourth heartbeat is used for the brain. This marvelous organ is encased in the skull and protected by cerebrospinal fluid. Some models of the brain can help us better understand its function.

Our inability to think clearly in some situations may be a result of brain structures that control us.

Emotional areas of the brain can suddenly and easily overpower logical thinking patterns.

At certain times in fetal development, neurons migrate to specific areas of the brain.

The brain accounts for only 2 to 3 percent of body weight, but it uses 20 to 25 percent of the body's energy!

The Triune Brain Model

The triune brain model, developed by neuroscientist Paul Maclean, was the first one that I was introduced to in the 1980s (see figure 3.1). Developed in the early 1950s, it has been used for educational purposes for the past 25 years. Although recent research has revealed that this model is too vague, it is still worth considering. It generally helps students understand how their brains function on a very simple level.

Maclean based the triune brain model upon the idea that the human brain has evolved over the years. During this evolutionary process, newer brains have been added onto the original brain, so that now we actually have three brains with which to process information (Hooper & Teresi, 1986).

Maclean's model divides the brain into three specific areas.

Figure 3.1. The Triune Brain Model

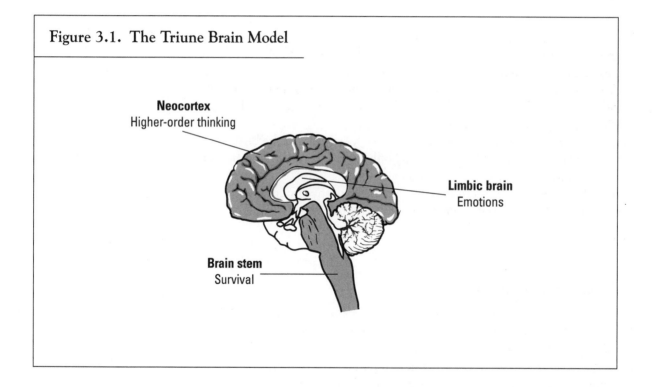

Neocortex
Higher-order thinking

Limbic brain
Emotions

Brain stem
Survival

The Brain Stem

Maclean's model begins with the oldest brain, called the *brain stem* or *reptilian brain*. The name *reptilian* comes from the idea that this brain was the first to develop and was similar to the brain of a reptile. It is not a thinking brain, but it deals with survival. All information passes through the brain stem before going to areas of the brain that deal with the higher levels of thinking. Maclean believes that any time you are in a fight-or-flight situation, your brain stem is in control of your body.

Is this an oversimplification? Absolutely. Children, however, have a much easier time understanding three levels of the brain as opposed to the multiple structures and layers that truly exist. You can tell them that their brain stem is the boss of the brain. It controls heart rate and respiration and takes over in times of undue stress or threat. This part of the brain does whatever it takes to ensure survival. Say, for example, you are crossing the street and suddenly see a large truck barreling toward you. Rather than examine the size, shape, or horsepower of the truck with higher levels of thinking, the brain stem takes over and causes you to run to safety.

> The triune brain model is easy for children to understand.

> The brain stem, or reptilian brain, deals with survival.

The Limbic Brain

The second level of Maclean's triune brain is the *limbic brain*, or the *mammalian brain*, so called because the limbic system relates to mammals other than humans. This part of the brain deals with emotion. The limbic brain has become one of the most important areas of the brain in current research. However, in this model it is another stepping-stone toward higher-order thinking.

> The limbic brain seeks to balance emotions.

The limbic brain houses structures that control eating, drinking, sleeping, hormones, and the emotions. Because of these duties, this area of the brain seeks homeostasis, or balance. Until this area has such balance, it will not allow information to flow to the highest level for logic and reasoning.

The Neocortex

The third and highest level of the brain in Maclean's model is the *neocortex*. This word literally means "new bark." It is the top level in this brain hierarchy and is in charge of all higher-order thinking. Here reading, planning, analyzing, synthesizing, and decision making occur. Students need to know that it is this level that is critical in a person's education. This is where the brain stores and retrieves educational "stuff."

> Higher-order thinking takes place in the neocortex.

Again, this model is far too simplistic for educators' purposes in understanding the brain. However, as a stepping-stone for teaching students about their brains, it works well. Many publications for children discuss this theory, and teachers indicate that their students have an understanding of their brains through this metaphor.

The Anatomy of the Brain

Let's look at the structure of the brain. Rather than look at all of the parts, we will look at only those that are pertinent to our discussion of how the brain learns.

The brain is divided into three sections: the hindbrain, the midbrain, and the forebrain (see figure 3.2). The hindbrain includes the cerebellum and the lower part of the brain stem. The midbrain covers the upper brain stem. The rest of the brain is considered part of the forebrain. Our discussion of the forebrain covers the limbic area, the thalamus, the hypothalamus, the hippocampus, the amygdala, the cerebrum, and the neocortex.

Figure 3.2. Sections of the Brain

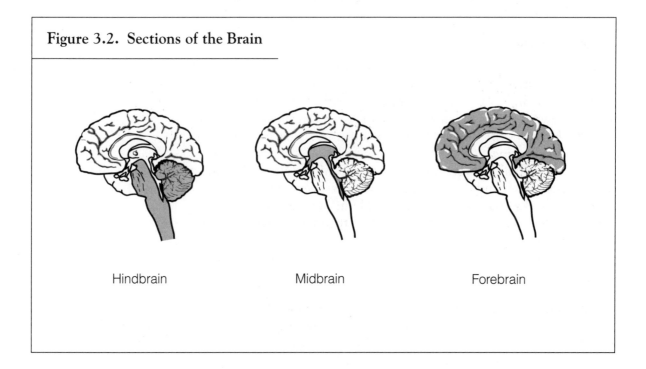

Hindbrain   Midbrain   Forebrain

The Hindbrain

The hindbrain controls the involuntary systems of the body.

The hindbrain controls the body's involuntary systems (see figure 3.3). All sensorimotor information enters the hindbrain via the brain stem. Within this structure resides another structure called the *reticular activating system* (RAS). The RAS regulates the amount and flow of sensorimotor information. It relays the information to the *thalamus*, a forebrain structure. The brain stem also contains the *pons*, which regulates dreaming and waking. The *medulla oblongata* is a hindbrain structure that controls heart rate and respiration.

At the very back of the skull, the *cerebellum* is attached to the brain stem and part of the hindbrain as well. The cerebellum has long been associated only with movement and balance. These important functions cannot be overlooked. However, researchers are studying the cerebellum to determine what other functions it performs. They have recently learned that the cerebellum stores a great many neurons and that this powerful piece of equipment has neural connections to many other brain structures (Leiner & Leiner, 1997). The cerebellum helps in memory formation. For decades researchers have known that the cerebellum houses procedural memory—what is sometimes called "muscle memory." Essentially this is our "how to" learning. How to ride a bike, how to drive a car, how to jump rope, how to swim, and so forth, are stored as memories in the cerebellum. Scientists have also discovered that the cerebellum is the site of memories of many learned situations that have become automatic but not necessarily associated with muscles. For instance, the cerebellum stores the alphabet after we learn it. Multiplication tables, the skill of decoding words, and the stimulus-response effects, such as knowing opposites (I say "hot" and you automatically say "cold"), are probably also stored here.

At the very back of the skull is the cerebellum, which aids in movement and balance.

The cerebellum stores procedural memories as well as many automatic memories.

Figure 3.3. The Hindbrain

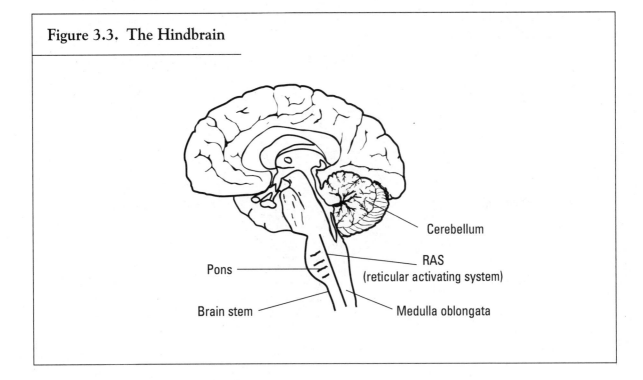

The Midbrain

Compared with the other areas of the brain, the midbrain is relatively simple. This very small area of the upper brain stem controls eye movement and the constriction of the pupils.

The Forebrain

The forebrain contains parts essential to learning.

From the reticular activating system, information goes to the thalamus, which sorts it and sends it to the specific areas of the brain.

As we ascend, we encounter the forebrain (see figure 3.4). This area covers the rest of the brain and contains parts essential to learning and memory. Here the information screened by the reticular activating system continues its journey through the mind. What happens to this information depends on the emotional, physical, and intellectual state of the learner.

The section of the forebrain containing interconnected memory and emotional structures is still called the limbic area. This area houses the walnut-sized *thalamus*. Most sensory information goes through the RAS to the thalamus, which sorts it and sends it to the appropriate places. Information processing is its major function, and it keeps the brain updated on what is going on in the outside world (Sylwester, 1995).

Figure 3.4. The Forebrain

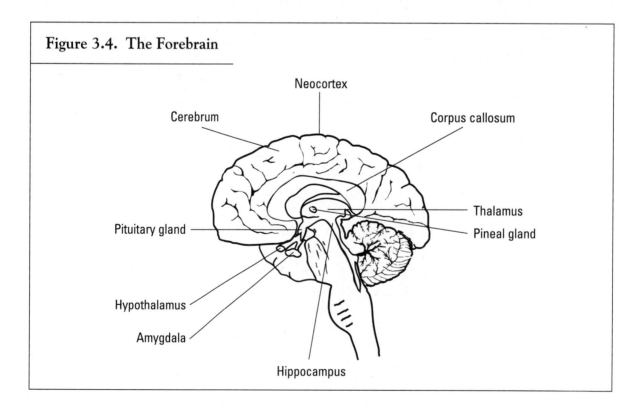

Above the brain stem and beneath the thalamus is the *hypothalamus*. This structure relays the information from within the body to the brain. Its job is homeostasis. For example, if your temperature is higher than 98.6 degrees Fahrenheit, your hypothalamus seeks ways to cool your body. Other roles of the hypothalamus include regulating sexual function and appetite control. Some recently advertised diet drugs affect the hypothalamus. The hypothalamus stays in close communication with the *pituitary gland*. This connection enables quick regulation of the body because the pituitary runs the endocrine system. This regulation includes adjusting the body's chemistry in a matter of milliseconds.

> Whereas the thalamus sorts information from the outside world, the hypothalamus sorts information from inside the body.

The *pineal gland* lies close to these structures. It regulates the release of neurotransmitters that regulate sleep. In hours of darkness it stimulates the release of melatonin, which brings on sleep. It is this regulatory system that may cause problems as travel across time zones changes a person's sleep schedule. Some people take over-the-counter melatonin tablets, and many report that after two or three nights of the medication, they are back on their regular sleep schedule.

> The pineal gland releases the neurotransmitters to regulate sleep.

Continuing on our tour, we find two structures that are crucial to learning and memory—the *hippocampus* and the *amygdala*. The hippocampus, shaped like a seahorse, functions as a filing cabinet for factual memories, storing both trivial and important information. As with most brain parts, there are two hippocampi—one in each of the brain's two hemispheres. This structure does not house all of your memories. It simply catalogs them and sends them for permanent placement in other long-term memory storage units (see Sylwester, 1997a). Without a hippocampus you cannot form new long-term factual memories. The hippocampus is comparable to a receptionist in a busy office. When you call the office and ask to speak to someone, the receptionist pushes buttons that connect you. If the receptionist is unavailable, you can dial the number and listen endlessly to the ringing. The person you want to speak to has no clue that you are calling. Of course, these days, there would be no receptionist. Instead a recording would answer and ask you to push the right buttons to connect yourself! In either case, the hippocampus is that person or machine relaying your calls.

> The hippocampus catalogs and files the factual information that the brain learns.

The amygdala resides next to the hippocampus. This almond-shaped structure is connected to many areas of the brain because it is in charge of emotional memory. Just as the hippocampus is the relay station for facts, the amygdala is the relay station for emotional information. The amygdala screens incoming information and determines if it is emotionally important for long-term storage. This very sensitive brain part is relevant in every information transmission. The amygdala's response to a situation can drastically affect the reaction to that situation. To teach my students

> The amygdala catalogs and files emotional information.

If you are watching a movie, your hippocampus remembers what you see and your amygdala remembers how you feel about it.

The top layer of the brain is the cerebrum. It is divided into two hemispheres.

The thin layer of material covering the cerebrum is called the cerebral cortex or neocortex.

the difference between the functions of the hippocampus and the amygdala, I use a metaphor. I tell them that the hippocampus tells them who the other boys and girls are, and the amygdala tells them whether they like them or not. That seems to cement their understanding of the differences.

The final structure to consider is the *cerebrum*. This top layer of the brain is divided, as most of the brain structures are, into right and left hemispheres. The two hemispheres communicate through a thick band of fibers, called the *corpus callosum*, that connects them. The cerebrum is covered by a thin layer of material called the *cerebral cortex*, or the *neocortex*. *Neo* means "new," and many consider this to be the newest layer of the brain in terms of evolutionary development.

The neocortex is about one-eighth of an inch thick, and if it were spread out it would be the size of a large piece of construction paper. Because it has to fold itself within our small skulls, it appears wrinkled. Actually, almost two-thirds of it lies within the folds. It is this cortex that is referred to as our "gray matter," even though it is actually pinkish brown. The rest of the cerebrum beneath the cortex is "white matter" and consists of axons, many of which have been myelinated, causing the white color.

The Information Trail

The cerebral cortex decides if factual information is to be stored. If so, it sends it to the hippocampus.

The cerebral cortex determines if emotional information is important. If so, it will send it to the amygdala.

Now that we've examined these major parts of the brain, let's follow some information through the brain. We take information into our brains through our five senses. That information is first filtered through the reticular activating system in the brain stem. Then it goes to the thalamus, the brain structure that sorts the information. By sorting, I mean that if the information is visual, the thalamus sends it to the visual part of the cortex; if it is auditory, it sends it to the auditory cortex, and so on. When information reaches the cerebral cortex, this higher area decides whether it should be acted upon or stored in long-term memory. If it is to be stored for the long term, the information is relayed from the cortex to the hippocampus, which catalogs and files it. If the information has emotional content, it is sent to the amygdala for a similar procedure.

This is how our memories grow. This is how we explore our world, make sense of it, and grow those dendrites. Sometimes, however, it does not happen exactly this way.

The Stress Response

You are at home with your best friend. She has convinced you to rent a video of the latest murder mystery. Usually you do not watch mysteries because when you were young, you had a very negative experience with an Alfred Hitchcock thriller. You have not taken a shower since seeing *Psycho*.

The popcorn that she brought you tastes great, so you settle in for a carefree afternoon of munching and watching. The plot is quite good, and you soon become more absorbed in the action on the screen and less interested in eating.

As the movie reaches its climax however, you notice that your heart is racing. The killer is approaching his final victim, and the police are nowhere near the scene of the soon-to-be crime. At first, you are frozen in your seat. Then as your hands become clammy, you don't even notice that the popcorn has slipped from your grip and spilled on the floor. Your stomach is churning, so you wouldn't care anyway. Just as you are about to either cover your eyes or run into the bathroom, the sirens blare, and the police show up in time. The star is saved, and your heart and breathing slow down.

What just happened to you? Let's trace the steps your brain went through in this situation. The information from the movie entered your brain through your brain stem. Your RAS decided how important it was and sent it to your thalamus for sorting. Your thalamus would ordinarily send the information to your neocortex to decide if it should be sent to the hippocampus for long-term memory. However, this information, especially because of your previous experiences with movies, was particularly emotional. Therefore, the amygdala jumped into the scene. It decided to act before the thalamus had a chance to send it anywhere. The amygdala declared an emergency! It contacted the hypothalamus and told it to send out signals to prepare your body for flight. Your hypothalamus contacted the pituitary gland, which sent out chemical signals to the adrenal glands located above your kidneys. Your adrenal glands released adrenaline and other peptides, such as cortisol. Your body started sending blood away from your digestive tract and to your legs and arms to prepare them for fight or flight. Your heart raced to get that blood flowing. This stress response can save your life (Sapolsky, 1994). Here, it kept you on the edge of your seat.

Many people would find this an exhilarating experience. In fact, they pay a lot of money at the theater for the experience. For you, it probably was not much fun because of the fear replicated from your experience with earlier movies.

This response is what made me act crazy in that grocery store. The stress chemicals that are released can affect your other thought processes.

Margin notes:

A stressful situation may cause the heart to race, blood flow to change, and respiration rate to rise.

A stress response can be triggered before the cerebral cortex has had the opportunity to examine the situation.

The amygdala initiates the stress response, causing the release of the stress chemicals that block thinking.

The stress response can save your life, or it can cause embarrassment.

Stress and Downshifting

Stress chemicals can block the neurotransmitters that are trying to make logical connections in your brain. This common occurrence is sometimes called "downshifting." It is the brain changing from a higher level of thought to a lower level (Hart, 1983). When I entered the store, I was using my neocortex to decide where to go and what to buy. The fear of who would recognize me caused my brain to shift down from my neocortex to my limbic area, where my emotions and my survival instincts took over.

People who are continually under stress may have some damage to their brains. When the stress chemicals are released, they cause problems for the hippocampus. Cortisol in particular can be destructive. It may remain in the body longer than other stress chemicals such as adrenaline. The consistent presence of cortisol has a toxic effect on the hippocampus—the filer of long-term factual memories (Jensen, 1998).

Some stress can be positive because it helps us find solutions to somewhat inconsequential problems. For instance, the rapid heartbeat and clammy hands that one may have on a first date are relatively harmless. This is also the case for job interviews, oral presentations, and trips to the dentist. If high levels of stress are a daily occurrence, the situation is different. For instance, a child who is abused physically or sexually may constantly be in a state of fear. This could cause some memory problems if the hippocampus has been physically damaged. Such a condition may also cause damage to neurons (Khalsa, 1997).

> Your students walk into your room, busily talking to each other about the carnival this evening. The girls are discussing what they are going to wear; the boys are bragging about how much money they have to spend on the games. Getting them to settle down is difficult. You lose your patience. In a booming voice you announce, "Take out a sheet of paper. We're going to have a pop quiz."
>
> Your students are suddenly attentive. They shift gears and have all but forgotten about the carnival. Quickly, you prepare a 10-question quiz off the top of your head. You have covered the material for the last week; your students should know it well.
>
> When the quiz is over, you collect the papers and rapidly score them. The results are disappointing. Your students' scores are below average! Now you are angrier. You yell at your students and tell them that because they are not paying attention they must review the material again. You assign 20 questions from the end of the chapter and tell them it will serve as a refresher for the week. They must finish in class because the carnival is this evening, and you don't want them to have homework.

Some stress chemicals remain in the body for long periods of time.

Although some stress can be positive, too much can damage the hippocampus.

We may not realize how easily we trigger the stress response in our students.

We must be aware of our own responses to stress in our classrooms.

What happened here? Everyone began operating from a stress response. Whether they had been using the neocortex or had been in the emotional area, they shifted to negative emotions of fear and maybe anger. You did this because you became angry. You were not using higher-order thinking skills when you threw that pop quiz at them. You may have been experiencing a lack of control and were trying to get it back. Your students immediately went from feeling excited and happy about the upcoming carnival to feeling fearful about an unknown quiz. They could no longer access their higher-order thinking areas. The poor test results caused you to react again from an area of stress, so you assigned the extra work. Any guesses what that did to your students? Their fear of not finishing and their anger with you could have kept many of them from accessing the particular brain areas they needed for the assignment. They remained in the limbic area with their emotions rather than reaching the neocortex and their thinking and memory skills.

> Pop quizzes may easily trigger a stress response in students.

Although much about the brain is unknown, some things are relatively easy to understand. We know that the neocortex is where we think, plan, remember, organize, and formulate sensible answers to problems. We know that the limbic area of the brain is where we deal with our feelings. *Those feelings will always take priority over anything else.* In the book *Emotional Intelligence*, Daniel Goleman (1995) discusses the impact that emotional intelligence has on the success of children throughout their lives. He includes abilities such as controlling one's own emotions, understanding others' emotions, and delay of gratification as important components of this type of intelligence. Because our emotions may very well be the force behind what we pay attention to, it is crucial that educators understand and deal with emotions first (Sylwester, 1997a).

> Emotions will always take priority over anything else.

> To get students' attention, we must first deal with their emotions.

Examining the Hemispheres

As mentioned earlier, the cerebrum is divided into two hemispheres. Each hemisphere is responsible for movement on the opposite side of the body. That is, the right hemisphere controls the left side of the body, and the left hemisphere controls the right side. Remember that communication between the two hemispheres takes place through the band of nerve fibers called the corpus callosum. The hemispheres may look identical, but they are dissimilar in both size and function.

> The right hemisphere of the brain controls the left side of the body, and the left hemisphere controls the right side.

Perhaps you have heard stories about "right-brained" people and "left-brained" people. These are simply that—stories. People are not "right brained" or "left brained" unless, of course, they have had a hemisphere removed. This type of surgery is done, but only under the rarest of circumstances. We use our whole brains to function.

> There are no "left-brained" or "right-brained" people. Each of us uses our whole brain.

Much of what researchers have discovered about the hemispheres is a result of surgeries in which the corpus callosum was severed. From these split-brain surgeries, neuroscientists discovered the separate responsibilities of each hemisphere (Restak, 1995). The left hemisphere is able to analyze; it deals with parts. The right hemisphere deals with wholes. The left hemisphere attends to spoken language, and the right hemisphere attends to body language. Analyzing music would occur in the left hemisphere and enjoying it in the right. The left hemisphere is sequential and time oriented, and the right is more spatial and lacks the time component.

You meet a person for the first time. After a short conversation you part company. As you walk away you think about what your new acquaintance said. You decide that this could be your new best friend. Your left hemisphere analyzed the words spoken. Your right hemisphere analyzed the tonality, tempo, volume, body language, and perhaps the attitude displayed. The two sides agreed that this was someone with possibilities as a future friend.

The Lobes of the Brain

Each of the brain's hemispheres is further divided into four lobes: *occipital, temporal, parietal,* and *frontal* (see figure 3.5).

The two occipital lobes (one for each hemisphere) are at the back of the brain. They process visual information. When visual stimuli are relayed from the thalamus, the information is sent to these lobes. Here it is processed, and recognition of seen objects occurs.

The two temporal lobes are located at either side of the head around the ears. These lobes are responsible for hearing. They also play a role in speech, learning, and memory. The upper back edge of this lobe is called *Wernicke's area*. Here thoughts are changed into spoken words.

The two parietal lobes are located on the top of the head toward the back. Each parietal lobe receives sensations from the opposite side of the body. The front of the parietal lobe is called the *sensory strip*. This is where the brain receives feedback in the form of pain, pressure, temperature, and touch.

The two *frontal* lobes take up a great deal of brain space. Each aids in critical thinking, problem solving, planning, and decision making. An area in the frontal lobe called *Broca's area* is responsible for putting spoken words in order. At the rear of the frontal lobe is the *motor strip*. Here voluntary movement is controlled. The left motor strip controls the right side of the body, and the right motor strip controls the left side. The front portion of the frontal lobe is called the *prefrontal* lobe. This is the area to which many researchers refer when they describe higher-order thinking.

Although the hemispheres have different functions, we use both sides of our brain in most situations.

Each hemisphere is divided into four lobes that have specific functions.

Thoughts are changed into spoken words in an area called *Wernicke's area. Broca's area* is responsible for putting spoken words in order.

The prefrontal lobe is where higher-order thinking takes place.

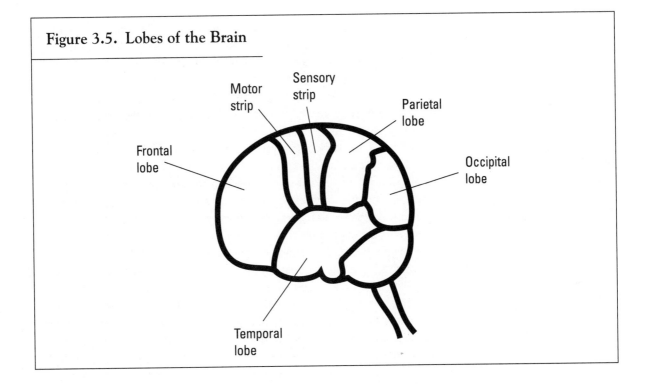

Figure 3.5. Lobes of the Brain

Lobe Development and Learning

If, as discussed in chapter 1, the frontal lobes are the last areas to receive a myelin covering, it is important to understand the effects this has on development. Our job as educators is difficult because we must teach to all levels of brain development. We must provide opportunities for higher-level thinking for those who are ready, and we must provide concrete experiences for those students who are more inclined to learn in this way.

We must consider not only development of the lobes, but also development of the emotions. Students who enter our classrooms living in the limbic area and operating from the stress response have different needs from those who don't.

As we face our classrooms every day, this basic understanding of the brain can help us focus on what is important. Every educator needs to know the facts being gathered on brain development and function. Through this information we can work toward a better understanding of learning and memory.

> The development of each area of the brain must be considered as we decide what to teach and how to teach it.
>
> Through an understanding of development and function of the brain, we can work toward an understanding of learning and memory.

The 30 children shuffle into your room at different paces. Some are walking briskly to their seats, taking out their materials, looking around

Each year we face another set of challenges as we teach students who are at different stages of brain development.

the room for any information about what the day will bring, and saying hello to their friends. Several are interacting with fellow classmates of the opposite sex; they are flirting and laughing—not interested in your agenda, but nonetheless happy to be here. Two or three dash to their seats just as the tardy bell rings. They are grateful to have escaped the possibility of demerits or detentions. They flip open their notebooks and look around for direction.

A boy in the back of the room is slouching in his chair, and his eyes are closed. You smile and nod, knowing that he was up late last night again. You will be lucky if he can focus at all. Two rows down you see Amy. Her boyfriend broke up with her yesterday. Those blue eyes remain puffy from all the tears. You offer a smile, but she looks down in pain. Gary's alcoholic parents are on a binge again. He is staying with the neighbors. Their new baby kept him up all night. In the center of the room sits Andy. The request you made for testing for special services is still being circulated. He tries so hard and seems to get nowhere.

This is it. The beginning of another day. You face not a classroom of 30 students, but 30 different individuals in a classroom. No two have come to you with the same backgrounds, the same experiences, or the same desires. No two have come with the same dendritic growth, myelination, or lobe development. They have all come with the same need to learn and remember.

4

Strolling Down Memory Lanes: Memory and Storage Systems

My two children will be arriving from their respective universities tonight for the Thanksgiving holiday. I have had an unusually long day at school, and I still have a 5 o'clock meeting to attend. I am rushing to the grocery store to stock my kitchen with the foods my children like.

My time is limited, and I am scurrying through the grocery store tossing items into my basket. I am very familiar with the layout of the store because I shop here often. As I reach the last aisle in the store, I realize that I have missed several items along my route. I ask myself, "Where is the pancake mix?" (Daughter Marnie loves pancakes.) I begin my search as I glance at my watch and conclude that I have only minutes to complete my shopping and get to my meeting on time. Okay, the mix must be in the aisle with the baking items. No luck. Well, then, it must be with the breakfast cereal. No, not there. Now I am not only perplexed, but also feeling some stress because of my time constraints. Where is the darn pancake mix?

Of course, I could ask someone. I look around. There is no help to be found. Okay, I guess I'll just go down all these aisles. I look at my watch again. If I am not out of here in 10 minutes, I'll be late for the meeting. My cart and I accelerate. My heart is racing as I think about Marnie's disappointment if I do not find the mix, and the disapproving looks from my committee members if I walk in late. "Why in the world did I agree to this meeting on this of all nights?!" As I zoom down the aisles, the food passes by in a blur. Am I really able to see what is here?

The 4:30 time on my watch causes an alarm to go off in my head. That's it! I have no more time. Sorry, Marnie. Maybe bacon and eggs will have to do! I dash to the checkout lane and unload my cart as my heart still beats wildly.

Memories can be affected by the time constraints that we place on ourselves.

Trying to do too many things at once may cause the brain to refuse to cooperate.

Locating memories may be impossible if we aren't looking in the right place.

Why did I have so much trouble shopping that day? I was in some unfamiliar territory. I knew where the items were that I usually buy, but I had to find several unusual items. The fact that I was under time constraints and that I had thousands of items to search through caused me stress and confusion. I thought I had finally covered the entire store, and I was upset that I never did look in the right place.

Just as the supermarket has different aisles for different food items, our brain has at least five memory pathways—semantic, episodic, procedural, automatic, and emotional—that it can use for permanent storage of information. Two other processes—short-term memory and working memory—are part of our memory system. We know where the memory processes begin, but scientists are still studying exactly how they work. Recall that the only evidence we have of learning is memory. It has been said that people "lose" their memories and that some of us have "good" memories and others have "poor" memories. To better understand these popular notions, let's take a closer look at what memory is all about.

Learning and Memory

For years students in psychology classes were taught that there were two kinds of memory—procedural, for how-to processes like riding a bike; and declarative, for things that can be recalled and reported. Then declarative memory was further defined as containing two categories—semantic, or word memory; and episodic, memory oriented to location. Researchers also referred to some temporary processes called either working memory or short-term memory. Some people called one or both of these processes conscious memory. These terms were sometimes used interchangeably, and not very effectively when it came to understanding the brain. Little was known of how or where memory was stored in the human brain.

Today's advanced technologies give us a much better idea of what is going on in our heads. Through the use of positron emission tomography (PET) scans and functional magnetic resonance imaging (fMRI), scientists can see the brain while a person performs different tasks; they can see information being stored and being retrieved. They can see which area of the brain is in use for different functions.

Neuroscientists have discovered that there are more storage areas than were originally thought. Although there is still more to discover, educators and others can use the information generated so far to help in the learning and memory process.

Research has shown that the five memory lanes begin in specific brain areas. These areas can be compared to those supermarket aisles, to filing cabinets, or perhaps even to computer floppy disks. The memory lanes

Just as stores have special areas for their products, the brain has special places for specific memories.

The brain has at least five different memory lanes.

The only evidence we have of learning is memory.

Current research suggests that there are more types of memory than just procedural and declarative.

contain the files in which memory is stored. The memories themselves are not in these areas, but the areas are where each memory is labeled. This labeling process makes the difference in how quickly we store and retrieve information.

Recall that learning occurs when neurons communicate with each other. Because we have up to one hundred billion neurons, there must be a way to reach the neurons containing the learning we are trying to retrieve. When we go to the grocery store to buy milk, it makes no sense to search for it in the bakery aisle. We could spend the entire day in that aisle and never find the milk. So it is with memory. If we choose the correct aisle for a particular memory, it won't take long to find it. In fact, we will probably find some related memories as well. I was using what I thought was related information to find the pancake mix. I looked in the aisles labeled Baking and Cereal in hopes of finding my product. I obviously had chosen the wrong labels, but I was using related information—a strategy that might work another time. Understanding memory and using strategies or mental models that allow us to access information are all part of learning.

Temporary Storage:
Short-Term Memory and Working Memory

I am in the front office at school looking up the phone number of a child's parent on the emergency card. I read the number to myself and turn to pick up the phone. The secretary has just answered a call and is talking. I check the clock and see that my planning period will be over in seven minutes, so I walk to the teachers' lounge to make my call. If I take the card with me, I will not have time to return it before class. I have no pencil, so I cannot write the number down. I rely on my memory and glance at the number for the final time: 452-3761. I walk quickly (no running allowed) down the hall, repeating the number over and over in my mind. My lips move as I say the number. I walk into the lounge and see another teacher using the phone. I glance at the clock. It is 1:28. Now, was that number 452-3761, or 452-3728? I should never have looked at that clock!

The science teacher hangs up the phone and says, "Sorry, I had to call Johnny's mother. Can you believe he got a 62 on his chapter test?"

I reach for the phone. 452-37 . . . 37 . . . was that 61 or 62? I slam down the phone and drag myself to my room. I guess I will make the call later.

The brain has more storage areas than originally believed.

If we know which areas hold specific memories, they will be much easier to find.

We have separate storage areas for permanent memories and temporary memories.

We have all experienced the frustration of quickly forgetting names and numbers.

Short-term memory has a time span of only 15 to 30 seconds.

The brain has limited space for short-term items.

Beginning at age 3 a child has one memory space. One is added every other year until the developmental age of 15.

Whereas short-term memory lasts for seconds, working memory can last for hours.

Dealing with information repeatedly may not place it in long-term memory.

That phone number never quite made it to my long-term memory. I had that number in a temporary storage area in my brain called short-term memory. Items in short-term memory last only a matter of seconds, usually between 15 and 30. That does not mean that it is not an effective memory to use. In fact, we use it all the time. Many memories must go through what Joseph LeDoux (1996) calls *short-term buffers*—temporary storage areas located in each of the auditory, visual, and kinesthetic areas—before they can go to working memory and then to long-term memory. Some researchers, such as Alan Baddeley (1990), have studied the components of short-term memory. According to Baddeley, we have only a few seconds to hold on to auditory signals, like the telephone number. As I repeated the number over and over, I reinforced those signals. Baddeley believes that we can hold pictures in our short-term memory for about five seconds. If we "say" to ourselves what is in the picture, we reinforce the visual memory with the auditory component.

Short-term memory has its limitations. Several researchers have discovered that we have limited "memory space" for short-term memory. This is actually a developmental phenomenon. The older you are, the more spaces you have for short-term memory. According to the work of George Miller and followed by that of Baddeley, adults (those who have reached a mental age of 15) can hold up to seven items in short-term memory (LeDoux, 1996). Beginning at age 3 a child has one memory space. Every other year this increases by one space until the capacity of seven is reached. Then two spaces can be either added or subtracted, depending on interest level and prior knowledge.

Another kind of temporary memory is called working memory. It is located in the prefrontal cortex, and it can be used for hours. It gives us the ability to form more long-term memories. An educational consultant, David Sousa (1995), points out working memory as having a longer time span than short-term memory.

Jennifer is a 7th grader. She is a fairly good student. Tomorrow she must take a social studies test. She pays attention in class, has taken good notes, and is just beginning to study. Jennifer reads over her notes several times. She looks for information in her social studies book and reviews it. She spends an hour studying for her test. Her mother quizzes her two or three times and decides that Jenn is ready for the test.

The next morning Jennifer takes out her notes. She does not feel as confident as she did the night before and begins reviewing again. This information is not very important to her, but her grade is very important to her and to her parents. After 15 minutes of studying, Jenn gets ready for school.

Social studies is her second-period class. She sneaks her notes out during her first-period math class and continues to review. She begins to get some facts mixed up in her mind and is tempted to write a few things on the palm of her hand but decides not to. The bell ending first period rings. She takes a deep breath, gathers her materials, and heads for social studies.

As she enters the classroom, all of the students are buzzing with facts that might be on the test. Jennifer sits down, closes her eyes, and tries to organize her thoughts. Mrs. Reed, the teacher, begins to pass out the test. The questions are a combination of multiple choice, matching, and short essay.

Jennifer passed her test. In fact, she did quite well. What Jennifer did was cram for her test. This method of studying puts information into her working memory. The information was repeated often enough in the 12 or so hours before the exam that it remained there. The confusion Jennifer felt was a result of not truly anchoring the information to prior knowledge or allowing the material itself to form "hooks" in her brain. Although she did well on the test, her brain soon disposed of the information because it was not put into long-term memory.

This method of cramming is how many of us got through school. It is effective for the moment, but it does not provide meaningful information that remains in the brain as neural networks to which connections can be added. A few bits of the information may have become meaningful for Jenn, but most of it did not. Think back to your classes and your tests. How much of the material you studied could you access now?

Permanent Storage: Long-Term Memory

Long-term memory consists of information stored for an indefinite period. Some researchers believe that the brain will dispose of memories that are not accessed. Others believe that we never lose our long-term memories, but we do lose our ability to find some of them. If you can't remember your friend's address, that doesn't mean she doesn't live there anymore.

I stated earlier when describing short-term memory buffers that information can be visual, auditory, or kinesthetic. Let's look more closely at these. In discussing the brain lobes, we learned that visual information is stored in the occipital lobe at the back of the brain; auditory information is processed and stored in the temporal lobe on the sides of the brain around the ears; and kinesthetic information is stored at the top of the

---

Repetition may hold items in working memory long enough to pass a test.

We have all had the experience of cramming for an exam.

If information is not meaningful or allowed to form patterns in the brain, it will be lost.

The brain is always seeking meaning.

brain in the motor cortex until completely learned and then permanently stored in the cerebellum, the area below the occipital lobe. Each of these areas has what is called an *association cortex*, which holds the information temporarily until it is either disposed of (forgotten), sent to working memory, or sent back to long-term memory.

New information goes into the brain by way of the senses. Those of us who prefer visual information may have more neural networks in our visual cortex than others who favor auditory information. How we prefer to receive information is important; and, in the memory process, how we retrieve it is even more important.

Information is retrieved from the brain area in which it is stored, and it is brought to the corresponding association cortex. The brain then may drop the information or send it to working memory where it is sorted and perhaps connected with other information.

For learning to be permanent, it has to follow certain paths. I call these paths "lanes." As mentioned earlier, there are five of them: semantic, episodic, procedural, automatic, and emotional. They are like those supermarket aisles. If I use the right one, I'll find my pancake mix. Each of the five memory lanes has a gateway to access the memory. These gateways are located in several areas of the brain that have been described in previous chapters. The gateways lead to information that has been stored in long-term memory. Scientists have discovered that even birds have multiple memory lanes. They store the memory of hiding places for food in one area of their brain and the memory for songs in another (Pinker, 1997). Is it any wonder then that humans have at least five memory lanes?

The memory lanes are categorized as containing either explicit or implicit memory. Explicit memory is voluntary. Its files are stored in the hippocampus, and it deals with memories of words, facts, and places. Both semantic and episodic memories are explicit. Implicit memory is involuntary. In other words, it is a compulsive response to a stimulus or a situation. The implicit memory system includes the procedural, automatic, and emotional memory lanes.

Semantic Memory

Semantic memory holds information learned from words. Most classroom situations rely heavily on semantic memory. We get semantic information from textbooks and lectures.

New information enters the brain through the brain stem, goes to the thalamus, and is then sent to the hippocampus, which is the file cabinet for factual memories. Just as the aisles at the supermarket have signs that tell us where items are located, the hippocampus has the signs or files for our memories. If incoming sensory information is factual, it will trigger

Information sent to the different lobes of the brain is held in the association cortex for that area.

When memories are retrieved, they are brought back to the association cortex.

The five memory lanes are semantic, episodic, procedural, automatic, and emotional.

The memory lanes contain either implicit or explicit memories.

Most classroom presentations rely heavily on semantic memory.

the hippocampus to search its files for matching information.

The hippocampus will bring information into those short-term buffers—temporary storage areas in each lobe—to be examined. If that information connects to the new information, it will be sent to working memory in the prefrontal cortex. Working memory will continue to sort and sift the old and the new material. Through prior knowledge or interest, the new information may be added to the old and form more long-term memory. This process may have to be repeated several times before long-term memory is formed.

The brain will process some of this information during sleep. Studies have shown that while rats are in the sleep stage called REM (rapid eye movement) sleep, their brains reproduce the same patterns used for learning while awake (Jensen, 1998). This may explain why last-minute cramming for tests may be so ineffective for long-term learning.

This memory lane is a difficult lane to use for learning because it takes several repetitions of the learning to cement it into the pathway. It has to be stimulated by associations, comparisons, and similarities. In short, semantic memory can fail us in many ways.

> You are watching television. On your favorite soap opera, the star is reading a book as she waits for her lover to return from his trip. Seeing her book reminds you that you have a library book that may be overdue. As soon as the commercial comes on, you get up to find the book. You reach the door to the study and suddenly wonder why you have come to this room. You simply cannot remember why you left that cozy spot on the couch and your favorite soap!

Your semantic memory has failed you. The soap opera scene triggered it. You had the association in your short-term memory along with the memory of your library book. The information simply did not remain in your memory long enough for you to find the book and check the due date.

Semantic memory obviously has its drawbacks, but it also has some good points. The hippocampus has a wealth of files just waiting to be opened. It also has an unlimited capacity to store new information. The proper associations can open up any of those files and help you retrieve the factual information that you have stored.

Episodic Memory

Accessing the episodic memory lane is easier. Episodic memory deals with locations. It is sometimes called contextual or spatial memory. The important link for this memory lane is that you are always somewhere

Semantic information must be repeatedly processed for long-term storage to take place.

Semantic memory must be stimulated by associations, comparisons, and similarities. It can easily fail us.

The hippocampus has a wealth of files containing information and an unlimited storage capacity for more information.

when you learn something, so you can easily associate the learning with the location. The gateway to the episodic memory lane is in the hippocampus. Remember that the hippocampus stores all factual information, and location is factual. It is almost as though this brain area has two file drawers—one for semantic memories and the other for episodic memories.

For instance, many of us who are old enough to remember when President John F. Kennedy was shot may ask each other the question, "Where were you when you found out about the assassination?" Younger people may relate better to the *Challenger* disaster or to Princess Diana's death.

The point is that we all remember some information because it is related to a location. The car that you drive when you are first learning how to drive will be easier for you to drive than other cars. Even though most cars have similar designs, you will remember your instruction and associate it with this particular car. Taking your driving test in another car will make the experience more difficult.

Researchers have conducted many studies to prove how important episodic memory is. Students who learn information in one room and take a test in another consistently underperform. Episodic memory has an important component called "invisible information." Students have more trouble solving math problems in English class than they do in their math classroom. Why? The walls, desks, overheads, chalkboards, and even the math teacher are covered with invisible information. The content of the room becomes part of the context of the memory.

If you were to walk back to the television room and your soap opera, you might look around hoping something in the room would trigger your memory. This is an effort to use the episodic memory lane to find information. In many instances, this works. However, episodic memory can be contaminated easily. Because you have had so many experiences and built so many memories in your television room, it is easy to be confused.

Procedural Memory

This memory lane has often been called "muscle memory." Information found when strolling down this lane deals with processes that the body does and remembers. Your ability to ride a bike, skip rope, roller skate, ski, and drive a car reside here.

The part of the brain that stores this information is the cerebellum. For years scientists believed that this brain structure was used solely for balance and posture. Recent research is suggesting that the cerebellum is doing much more than ever imagined (Leiner & Leiner, 1997). We now know that its work includes procedural memory. A procedure is stored in the cerebellum at the time it becomes routine.

Episodic memory is also called contextual or spatial memory.

We remember some information because it is related to a location.

Students who learn information in one room and are tested in another room score lower than students who are taught and tested in the same room.

One interesting component of episodic memory is the invisible information that it contains.

Procedural memory is often called muscle memory.

Not only was your episodic memory storing information when you first learned to drive, but your procedural memory was also activated. Procedural memory stored the sequence used in driving. The procedure of stopping at a red light, hitting your brakes when you see brake lights in front of you, and turning the wheel to round corners and avoid collisions all reside here.

The storage of procedural memory has given humans the ability to do two things at once. The fact that we can drive cars and talk on the telephone at the same time is an example of this. Because these functions require two distinct areas of the brain, they do not fight for brain space or energy. They can be done simultaneously. (Extra care must be taken if you do both of these simply because the brain can shift attention easily.)

Trying the procedural memory lane is an excellent choice for your next attempt at remembering why you left the television room. Returning to that comfortable position on the couch might bring back the memory. It sometimes helps to just get into the same position and do whatever you were doing. Many people have easier times remembering something they learned standing up if they just stand up to trigger the memory.

Automatic Memory

Automatic memory, identified just recently, is often referred to as *conditioned response memory* (Jensen, 1998). Certain stimuli automatically trigger the memory or information. It could be a song that is playing. After you hear the first few words or the opening notes, you begin to sing the song. Automatic memory lanes are located in the cerebellum.

What might you already have stored in automatic memory? The alphabet, the multiplication tables, and probably your ability to decode words. That means that your ability to read—but not to comprehend—is in your cerebellum. Lots of songs may be stored there as well. Any learning that has become automatic for you may be stored in your automatic memory. Sets of words such as *stop and go, black and white, up and down,* and *in and out* are stored here. If you practiced learning information using flash cards, that material is stored in your automatic memory.

Your automatic memory may cause other memory lanes to open. For instance, you hear a song that you haven't heard in a long time. You begin to sing the song. As you are singing, you remember the last time you sang that song. You remember that you were on your way to visit a friend in the hospital. Your episodic memory has been triggered. You picture yourself clutching the steering wheel of your blue Oldsmobile as you approached the hospital. You have activated your procedural memory. As you think about the hospital, you remember the name of the friend you were there to visit. Your semantic lane opened up with this factual information.

Procedural memory stores memories of the processes that the body does.

Sequences that are consistently repeated, like tying a shoe, are stored in procedural memory.

Automatic memory is sometimes called conditioned response memory.

Automatic memory contains decoding skills and multiplication skills but not comprehension skills.

Triggering one memory lane may activate other memory lanes.

Suddenly, you are crying as you remember how sad you felt that day about your friend's suffering. You have just entered your emotional memory.

Emotional Memory

The emotional memory lane is opened through the amygdala, located in the forebrain next to the hippocampus. Whereas the hippocampus files factual information, the amygdala stores emotional information. This filing cabinet holds files containing all sorts of experiences that made you happy or sad or any other feeling you can name.

Emotional memory takes precedence over any other kind of memory. The brain always gives priority to emotions. When information enters the brain and reaches the thalamus, the amygdala will grab that information if it is emotional and go straight to work on it. If the information calls for strong emotion, especially fear, the amygdala takes over to prepare the body. Daniel Goleman (1995) calls this response a "neural hijacking." At this point, no other memory lanes have a chance.

The amygdala may employ the stress response and cause all sorts of havoc. The release of stress hormones like cortisol may cause interrupted transmission of information in the brain and make it impossible to think clearly. All of the memory lanes could be blocked by these unwanted and sometimes dangerous chemicals.

Emotional memory may be triggered by another memory lane, and then it may take over the "logical" mind. For instance, you need to do some research for a project. You think about the need to make time to visit the local library to search the periodical files. Suddenly, as you picture the library through your semantic lane, you "see" in your mind the librarian, who is someone you cannot tolerate. Your anger and disgust "take over" your thinking. You may then decide to go to a different library, forget the research, or simply try to avoid her on your trip. Your behavior will depend on the strength of your feelings.

> As you gaze at the television, your favorite character becomes upset at the late return of her lover. She picks up her book and throws it. You think to yourself, "Of course, you are angry. You should throw more than that book! Book?! Book?! That's what I went into the study to get!"

In this case, your emotional memory activated your semantic memory again, and you have finally discovered the answer you have been seeking.

The memory lanes are located in specific areas of the brain (see figure 4.1). An understanding of the brain and of these lanes may help in understanding how people think and feel. Short-term buffers and working

---

Emotional memory is the most powerful kind of memory.

If your emotional memory takes over, you may lose all logic.

Emotional memories may cause the release of stress hormones that will "change" your mind.

The memory lanes are located in specific areas of the brain.

memory are temporary storage areas. Semantic, episodic, procedural, automatic, and emotional memory lanes are used to access and store information for long-term memory.

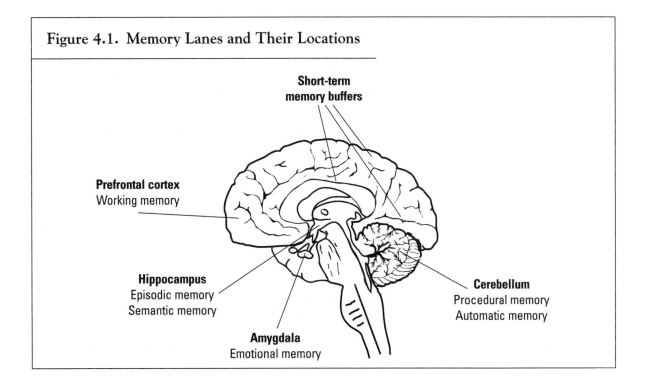

Figure 4.1. Memory Lanes and Their Locations

Short-term memory buffers

Prefrontal cortex
Working memory

Hippocampus
Episodic memory
Semantic memory

Amygdala
Emotional memory

Cerebellum
Procedural memory
Automatic memory

Mixing Messages

Research suggests that of all the forebrain structures, the hippocampus is the last to develop. Oftentimes, it is not working well until age 3 (Le-Doux, 1996). This is probably why so many adults have no memories of events that occurred before this age. Because the hippocampus is not developed, the brain does not store factual information. However, the amygdala is developed, and it is possible to store emotional memories. Remember that the hippocampus tells you who someone is, and the amygdala tells you how you feel about that person.

Have you ever felt blue and not known why? Many neuroscientists have studied this phenomenon. Some believe that the situation occurs because an emotional memory has been triggered, and the factual memory either does not exist or has not yet been triggered.

The hippocampus is the last forebrain structure to develop.

How can this be? If the emotional memory was stored before the hippocampus developed, there may be no factual memory associated with it (LeDoux, 1996). If the emotional memory occurred with the stress response in high gear, cortisol and other chemicals may have blocked the transmission of the factual memory. Sometimes this blockage is temporary, and sometimes it is permanent.

We may have emotional memories with no factual memories to explain them.

I once worked with someone who claimed to remember many events from her very early childhood. My colleagues and I spent many hours over the years listening to her stories from the ages of 1, 2, and 3. What I did not have the heart to tell her was that she was "telling stories." She was using her episodic memory lane and telling us stories that had been told to her dozens of times by her parents and others. After hearing this information time and again, she stored it as her own personal memory. Episodic memory can be dangerous because it is not always reliable in terms of details from the past.

Episodic memory may not always be reliable as time passes.

A New Wrinkle

We have learned that each day the brain prunes some neuronal connections because of lack of use. That may be the bad news, but the good news is really good! You don't have a bad memory. What you have are different memory lanes in which to store different types of memories. If you are having trouble accessing information, you may simply be searching the wrong lane. There is hope for all of us. And as research continues, memory-enhancing drugs are being developed. Will there come a time when we will all be taking our daily "cranium capsule"? It certainly is a possibility!

If you are having trouble accessing information, you may not be using the correct lane!

5

Where Is Wally?
Locating Memories in the Brain

I was a rather immature freshman in high school when I first heard his name—Wally. I thought it was a rather silly name; it made me think of "Leave It to Beaver." But even though I didn't like his name, he had a great smile. He would smile or pretend to grab my books as I walked down the science hall at Peoria High.

Wally had entered my heart. Well, actually, Wally had entered my brain.

Making Memories

We can learn something from every experience. The more memory lanes used for storage of an event, the more powerful the learning will be.

Now, let's see. Where had Wally entered my brain? First, he entered my semantic lane through my hippocampus. This is where that name was first stored. And, yes, he was already in my emotional lane through my amygdala. All kinds of neurotransmitters were released when he smiled at me. I have my first episodic memories of him from that science hall, although many of them are very dim. That's because some of those "Wally" neurons have been pruned away and replaced by other memories. Procedurally he is there, too. Walking down that hall with an armload of books would bring back an instant picture of him. Do I have an automatic memory of him, too? You bet—every time I hear the "Leave It to Beaver" theme song. Some would say that I had Wally on the brain!

If our relationship had ended with those small encounters, most of those memories would have faded and been replaced by other connections. However, the story continues.

Toward the end of my sophomore year, my longtime boyfriend, Steve, and I broke up. I was heartbroken for about 24 hours. Then Wally asked

Powerful memories from years past can be triggered by a present experience.

Over time, some neurons are pruned away and memories are forgotten.

The brain draws from many memory lanes to create and recreate memories.

Sights, sounds, and movements add to the richness of memories.

A simple action, such as walking up a flight of stairs, may become part of a memorable event.

Locations are often imbedded in our memories because we associate them with emotional events.

me for a date. For the next four months my brain grew "Wally" dendrites and strengthened "Wally" synapses. I can only imagine what my neurons looked like! But all good things must come to an end. Or so I was told later.

It was a typical Friday night—"guys' night out." So, of course, it also had to be "girls' night out." This particular Friday night I had a plan. I had no intention of spending my evening with the girls if I didn't have to. I was on a mission to spend another evening with Wally. After all, it was close to the end of the school year. Wally would be graduating soon and going away to college. Every minute was valuable.

I arranged to have my sister's car. I had to make all sorts of promises that I wouldn't keep to be able to drive the old red Chevy that night. It was somewhat difficult to explain to my friends that I wasn't going out with them. I somehow got the point across that Wally couldn't get his car, and I was hoping to end the evening with him.

Friday nights in Peoria usually meant a trip to Mayfair Hall. This dance spot was one of the main teen hangouts. My plan was to arrive at Mayfair after Wally and his friends had been there long enough to be ready to move on. My hope was that he would be tired of his friends and ready for some new company.

I arrived at Mayfair shortly after Wally. He was in the hall where music was blaring. There was hardly room to move, let alone dance. I made my way through dozens of teens down the dark staircase to the dance floor. Wally was laughing and talking to the guys. A few senior girls were hanging around them, and I was somewhat hesitant to approach. However, I didn't want all my planning to have been for nothing, so I reached out and touched his arm. He spun around, and I watched his smile fade.

"What are you doing here?" he yelled above the music.

"I thought you'd want to dance," I stuttered with a pounding heart.

"No. Let's go," he said rather gruffly and led me through the hall and up the dark stairs.

I began to hope that my plan had worked. In the parking lot, kids and cars were everywhere, and I searched faces, proud to be seen with "my" Wally. As we approached the car, Wally slowed his pace. He was staring at the pavement and shaking his head.

"Is something the matter?" I asked in a shaky voice.

"Yeah. I don't want to go with you," came his hurtful reply.

"Okay, go back down with your friends; I'll catch up with mine." I tried to sound cheerful—as though this was no great disappointment.

"No! You don't get it," he began. "I don't want to go out with you anymore. I'll be going away to school, and I don't want any attachments. Okay?"

My brain quit functioning at any level that remembers words or faces. I began functioning automatically. I know I left the parking lot in my sister's red Chevy. Alone. I immediately began to berate myself for pushing myself on him on a Friday night. Surely he would not have broken up with me if I had waited to see him on Saturday. I snapped the radio on and tried to figure out where to find the girls. If I returned home this early, my parents would be alarmed and bug me. My fingers started pushing the buttons for a soothing melody. The first song I heard was "Big Girls Don't Cry." I switched stations. In circumstances like this, the appropriate song always finds me. I landed on the station playing "Where Did Our Love Go?" by the Supremes. The rest of the evening is a blur.

Music can be a very powerful trigger for memories.

Retrieving Memories

My brain made many connections that night. All of my memory lanes were activated, and I can access that experience through all of them (see figure 5.1). This was very powerful learning.

It began as an emotional experience, and I can easily access it through the emotional memory lane. To open that storage file and retrieve the correct files of memories, the correct trigger must be squeezed. The trigger may be someone talking about high school, or it may be hearing others discuss their "lost loves." It could also be a conversation about painful experiences or the silly things one does as a teenager.

The most powerful learning takes place in multiple memory lanes.

The fact that I can write about the episode proves that it is also in my semantic memory. Remember that semantic memory is words. Discussing the topic with others draws from those factual memories stored through my hippocampus. A variety of words, such as *Mayfair Hall, Wally,* or *Bigelow Street* (Wally's street) may trigger these files.

Memories of important events and people reside in more than one part of the brain.

Whenever I hear either of the songs that was playing on the car radio that night, the memory is triggered through my automatic memory. This conditioned response was learned quickly but may never leave me. It is stored through my cerebellum along with my decoding skills for reading, my knowledge of riding a bike, and my multiplication tables. For years the songs were painful to listen to, but now they bring back both the good and the bad memories of Wally and high school.

Going down the street past Mayfair Hall may cause my episodic memory lane to activate. This memory is also stored through my hippocampus. Mayfair Hall is no longer open, but the building is still there to remind me of my past.

Returning to certain locations activates episodic memory.

Getting into an old red Chevy, walking down a dark stairway, or even entering a busy parking lot may open up my procedural memory lane to

Wally. This occurs less and less as time goes by because other procedures that are more commonplace are more easily activated through my cerebellum. My brain has slowly pruned away some of those "Wally" neurons as they are not used.

Recalling an emotional event may open all the memory lanes.

The point that my story illustrates is that strong learning took place with that experience. That learning entered all of the storage facilities in my brain. What caused all of those lanes to open? Remember that emotional memory will take priority over all other memories. This was definitely an emotional experience. When the emotional memory lane is triggered, we can expect other memory lanes to open. Active emotional engagement appears to be a key to learning. If there is no emotional engagement in a particular task, will learning still occur? The answer, thankfully, is yes. However, an outside force must stimulate the other lanes in order to open the files stored there. This is the most difficult task.

Active emotional engagement is a key to learning.

Powerful Learning

Let's look at another example. As I was driving to make a presentation, I listened to an audiotape of the book *The Giver* by Lois Lowry. I thought I

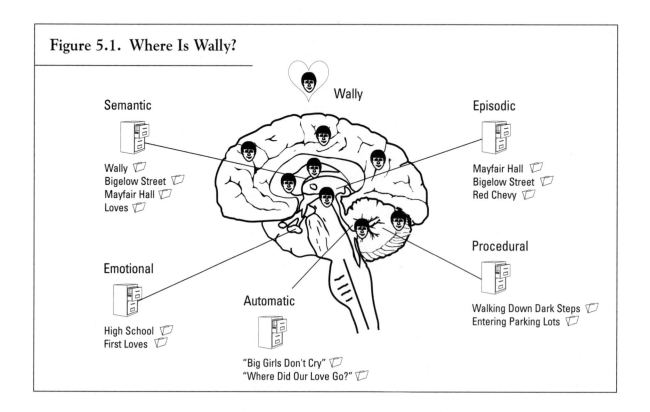

Figure 5.1. Where Is Wally?

Semantic

Wally
Bigelow Street
Mayfair Hall
Loves

Emotional

High School
First Loves

Automatic

"Big Girls Don't Cry"
"Where Did Our Love Go?"

Wally

Episodic

Mayfair Hall
Bigelow Street
Red Chevy

Procedural

Walking Down Dark Steps
Entering Parking Lots

might want to use the book with my 7th grade classes. Where is *The Giver* in my brain?

As I listened to the science fiction novel, three lanes immediately became activated. Episodic memory was activated because every time I learn, I am in a location. Therefore, if someone were to ask me questions about the novel, I would have better recall in my car. The semantic lane was activated as I listened and concentrated on the words. Because I did not read the words and I happen to be a visual learner, oral questions and answers might be much easier for me. The emotional lane was activated as I fell in love with the characters in the novel. I knew right away that I wanted to share this story with my students. Because I have been sharing this novel ever since that road trip, some memories are stored through my cerebellum and the automatic memory lane. Repetition enables me to respond automatically to certain situations and facts in the story, which I originally would have been unable to do.

Memory Failure: Where Are Those Darn Keys?

Let's consider an example familiar to all of us. Have you ever lost your keys? You didn't actually lose them, of course. You put them somewhere, and then you couldn't find them. If you had a ritual of walking into the house and putting your coat and keys in a particular place, they should always be in the same spot. Somehow, though, they disappeared. Perhaps you were holding extra items and placed the keys with those. Maybe the phone was ringing when you walked in, and you dashed to answer it. Something important may have been occupying your thoughts, and you neglected to follow your usual routine. Automatic memory failed you because you didn't follow the routine. (Actually, it didn't fail you; you failed it.) What do you try next?

Episodic memory sometimes works. You can go back to the places where you last remember having your keys. The information there may aid your memory. Maybe not.

You can then try the procedural lane. Actually pick up your coat and anything you believe you had with you. You might even go out to the car and literally retrace your steps. (If you are a visual learner, you could probably save steps by picturing the entire scenario.)

If all three of these memory lanes fail you, you still have other options. How about searching your semantic memory? That's right, use those higher-order thinking skills and ask yourself some questions. "What could have happened to my keys?" Now you are using both your working memory and your semantic memory to study the problem. "Maybe they fell under the table. Do I have a hole in my coat pocket?"

Episodic memory is easily activated because every time you learn something you are in a particular location.

Where did I put the car keys? At times, our memories seem to play tricks on us.

Most learning occurs in multiple lanes.

Systematically examining each memory lane may help you find your keys.

Emotional memory doesn't usually play a role in finding your keys even though you may become very emotional about the situation. Unless you have very strong feelings about your keys, you won't store their whereabouts through your amygdala. However, you may store this experience of misplacing them.

If you have engaged the stress response, it will become increasingly more difficult to find your keys. You may be better off asking for help or calling for a ride. When you have relaxed and your stress level goes down, your brain will function better.

So, sit down and take a deep breath. This allows oxygen to get to your brain to help you enter one of those memory lanes. You've probably already tried the easy ones, so now you need working memory to engage some long-term memories to help you sort things out.

We have been told for years that everything we experience is recorded somewhere in our brains. That just isn't so (Rose, 1993). Therefore, the "key" information may have filtered right out, and you will find your keys by searching as though they are someone else's keys. This is a tactic I have often used successfully. "If I were a set of keys, where would I be?" This actually helps me calm down, and I begin asking myself the questions I would ask someone else if their keys were missing.

As I get older, I fill my brain with information that is important to me. That's not to say that my keys aren't important, but I find myself paying attention to other things in my life. A result of learning about the memory lanes is knowing how and when to pause and examine what I am seeking and what might be the best way to reach my goal.

Memory's Effects

Our memories affect our decisions. We name our pets and our babies according to the connections we have with those names. The homes we buy are greatly affected by the memories we have of our previous homes and the homes of others with whom we have had contact. Our memories may also influence the careers we choose. That special teacher who made us feel good about ourselves may cause us to choose a career in education in order to help others. The fact that our father was never home because he started his own business, and we felt slighted by his absence, could influence our decision to stay out of the business world. Memories are powerful. They help us make decisions, affect our actions and reactions, and determine our course in life.

When the brain stores memories in more than one memory lane, they become even more powerful. Because learning is memory, and the only evidence we have of learning is memory, then the more memory lanes we

When emotions take over, it may be even more difficult to remember.

It is easy to forget the trivial things in our lives when a multitude of other things requires our attention.

Our memories greatly influence our lives.

When memories are stored in more than one memory lane, they become more influential.

use to store information, the more powerful the learning becomes.

As I finished this chapter late one evening, the phone rang. I answered the phone and received an apology. "I'm sorry for calling so late, but this is driving me crazy. For the past two days I keep seeing a gray house in my mind. It has white trim, and it's very small. Inside there are stacks of newspapers, and the house is a mess. Where am I?"

It is my sister, Linda, calling from her home in the Chicago area. Her semantic memories immediately trigger my episodic, emotional, and procedural lanes. "You're at that house (episodic) we all thought was haunted! That strange old woman (emotional) lived there. It was down the street and around the corner. We would always walk (procedural) through the overgrown grass and weeds in her lot to get to the Wheelers' house. Remember how you found that animal bone in her lot, and we were sure it was human?"

Linda sighs. She thanks me for relieving her agony over not being able to connect the information in her head. We laugh about the fact that the woman was probably not crazy, nor the house haunted. We say good-night. She climbs into bed to sleep peacefully. I dash to my computer to add this story before I forget it!

Our memories make us who we are. Without our memories, our very identities are in jeopardy. Our brain can easily store all learning experiences. Teaching to multiple memory lanes makes the connections to those experiences stronger and easier to access.

It is easy to get "stuck" in one lane. Accessing the other memory lanes requires another trigger.

Repeating things or writing them down may assist your memory.

Our memories confirm our existence.

6

The Path Most Traveled: Semantic Memory Instructional Strategies

The students hurry into the classroom. They take their seats quickly and appear impatient for me to begin. As I take attendance, I notice some students grabbing their notebooks and studying their vocabulary lists. Their eyes dart from the lists to the clock and then back to me.

Finally, a brave student says, "Mrs. Sprenger, please hurry before I forget!" I smile at him as I begin passing out the vocabulary tests. The students put their notebooks away, snatch the tests from my hands, and begin writing as fast as they can.

Are my students showing me their love of learning? No. They are simply giving me every indication that they have not learned their vocabulary words. They have simply been trying to repeat the information over and over in their minds for several minutes before the test. They are desperately trying to retain the words in their short-term and working memories long enough to pass the test.

This is a problem of epidemic proportion when students confront semantic information. When their brains do not process this type of information in different ways to make the neural connections in the semantic lane, many students try desperately to use the temporary storage processes to get by. In most cases, they are unsuccessful.

Using what you know about the five memory lanes makes it easier to plan lessons that access the lanes you desire. The most powerful learning comes from using all five lanes in your teaching and learning situations.

Let's look at strategies that are useful for accessing the semantic memory lane. Because the semantic lane calls on working memory, it requires

Students commonly try to hold information in short-term memory for tests.

When semantic information is not processed in several ways, the brain has a hard time making neural connections in the semantic memory lane.

Semantic memory operates word by word, and it uses working memory.

64

the most effort and is used more consistently in educational settings than the other lanes.

Semantic Strategies

Remember that semantic memory operates word by word, and it uses working memory. Therefore, each learning experience should be organized to present a short chunk of information. The brain must process the information in some way after the presentation of each short chunk. This processing may take many forms. Let's examine some of the devices you can use in your teaching to help students build semantic memories.

Graphic Organizers

Graphic organizers can help students retain semantic information. Mind mapping, or webbing, illustrates a main idea and supporting details. I call these devices "power pictures" because they paint such powerful images in your mind. This technique takes concepts and accesses the best memory lane to help you remember and store that information.

To make a mind map write an idea or concept in the middle of a sheet of paper. Draw a cloud around it. Then draw a line from the cloud. Using the same color as the color of the line, write a word or phrase to describe or support the central idea or concept. Use the fewest possible words to describe the concept. Then draw a picture or symbol to represent your description. Draw other lines coming out from the cloud in a similar fashion for other ideas or subtopics. Each line, word, and symbol should be the same color, but each set—representing the separate ideas or subtopics—should be a different color. The use of a symbol or picture brings emotion into the learning and helps access another memory lane—emotional memory—to enhance learning.

I use mind mapping when I teach the seven elements of the short story (see figure 6.1). Using the overhead projector, the class and I create the power picture. My students draw the power picture, or mind map, in their literature notebooks. We have fun creating the pictures and symbols. They laugh at my poor artwork. However, my poor artwork gives many kids the confidence they need to do their own drawings.

Creating mind maps has been a successful strategy for my students. They remember the seven elements much more readily than they did when I used other methods. Some students may remember the colors; some may remember the words; and some may remember the position of the information on the page.

The following strategies can help students remember semantic information:

graphic organizers
peer teaching
questioning strategies
summarizing
role-playing
debates
outlining
time lines
practice tests
paraphrasing
mnemonic devices

Graphic organizers are one of the most powerful ways to build semantic memories.

"Power pictures" are excellent graphic organizers.

Figure 6.1. A Power Picture

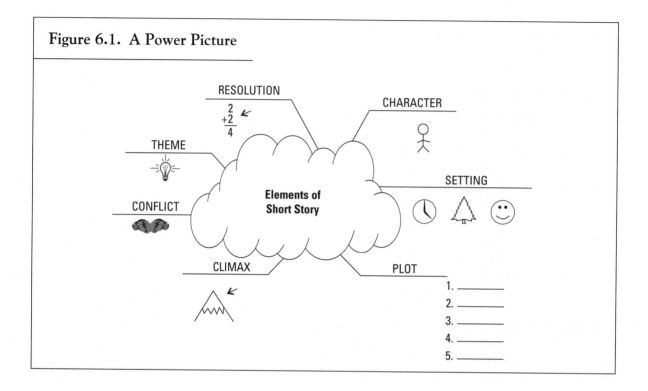

Peer Teaching

Peer teaching is a great way to build interpersonal skills and to review material. Many students love the idea of teaching. Pair up the students and have them take turns teaching the information just covered. This process gives them the opportunity to evaluate and synthesize the material. Evaluating and synthesizing are important higher-order thinking skills.

Questioning Strategies

Questioning sessions emphasize important pieces of semantic information. One way to approach this is to ask open-ended questions that give all levels of learners the opportunity for a "right" answer. Another approach is to provide the answers and have the students come up with the questions. A favorite strategy of mine in the literature classroom is to have the students come up with questions they would like to ask the characters. The questions themselves reveal their understanding of the literature, so there is no need for answers.

Giving answers and having students create the questions can be an interesting approach to triggering semantic memory.

Summarizing

Either you or the students can summarize. You can ask for one-sentence summaries. Give recognition to students who create concise sentences that are not run-ons or fragments. This often encourages other students, and as they listen to the summaries, the information is repeated. This repetition helps cement the information in the semantic lane.

Role-Playing

Time constraints make it impractical to do role-playing after each chunk of information is presented, and this strategy can get old. Assigning each team a chunk to role-play may solve the problem. In the case of a history lesson, students may role-play battles or military decisions. For literature, students enjoy acting out scenes from stories or novels.

Debates

Many students enjoy participating in and listening to debates. This may not work for all material, but it is a solid strategy for cementing semantic information. If students have to provide proof for their arguments, they are more likely to carefully analyze the information studied. Debating the reasons for the Civil War, character motivation, or alternative problem-solving methods are excellent ways for students to examine and study semantic information.

Outlining

Traditional outlining is an alternative to graphic organizers. Students whose thinking is linear and sequential will enjoy it, and students whose thinking patterns are not as linear should become familiar with this strategy. Putting students in groups of two or three may make learning this procedure more fun.

Time Lines

Time lines work well in some situations. For the semantic information in history, making time lines will put events in a logical sequence to make learning easier. In literature units, such as Greek mythology, time lines assist students in understanding the development of the families. This can be done as a class or in small groups. Student interaction can be essential to understanding the information.

Practice Tests

Practice tests can help students put information in the appropriate format for a traditional test. Semantic information that is placed in other

> Summarizing is a processing technique that calls on higher-order thinking skills.

> Role-playing and debate can access different memory lanes as students process semantic information.

> Some linear sequential thinkers may benefit from traditional outlining.

> Practice tests provide opportunities for students to transfer information to test format.

memory lanes must be practiced for standardized tests. This opportunity may be necessary to retrieve the information from other lanes and place it in the semantic lane. This can be a real boost to their final assessment on the material.

Paraphrasing

Paraphrasing is a strategy that will challenge some students and help many. Taking the author's words and putting them into "kid talk" may help many understand the material. Students can do this individually or in pairs or small groups. Begin by using this strategy orally, and then have students practice paraphrasing in writing. Comparing their perceptions with those of teammates or partners will add to their understanding of the material.

Mnemonic Devices

Mnemonic devices help build memories. Using them puts information into automatic and semantic memories. Peg systems, acronyms, rap, and music are just a few mnemonic devices that can increase memory and retention. They can also be fun.

Using the body as a peg system works for many people (see figure 6.2). A peg system often makes it easier to memorize a list. For example, if I have to learn 10 prepositions, I can use body parts to help me remember them. Starting at the top of my body, I tell a story, and as I move down my body I use the prepositions in order:

> When the fly climbed **aboard** my forehead, I noticed that he was **about** two inches from my nose. There was some peanut butter **above** my chin that I was sure he was interested in. I was surprised **after** he flew past my shoulder, **around** my elbow, and landed **beyond** my wrist **on** my hand. Then he buzzed **over** my hip **until** my knee hit him and he rested **under** my foot.

A rhyming peg system works well for me, and it is easy for my students to remember (see figure 6.3). I always introduce it to my students by first performing a "magic" feat. They are fascinated by this ability and even more pleased when I explain how it is done.

I stand with my back to the chalkboard, and I have one student go to the board and write a list of items suggested at random by the other students. For instance, we might list school supplies. The student compiling the list calls on students one at a time. The students call out both the item and the number on the list where it should be placed. A student might say, "Number four is a ruler." This continues until the list of 10 is complete.

Mnemonic devices can be fun for students and for teachers.

A body peg system may be a helpful mnemonic device for some students.

A rhyming peg system may be an easier mnemonic device for some students.

Students are surprised to see how successful they can be when they use some of these memory aids.

Figure 6.2. A Body Peg System for Memorizing Prepositions		
Number 1	forehead	aboard
Number 2	nose	about
Number 3	chin	above
Number 4	shoulder	after
Number 5	elbow	around
Number 6	wrist	beyond
Number 7	hand	on
Number 8	hip	over
Number 9	knee	until
Number 10	foot	under

The students must give me a moment between items, so I can take the time to "attach" them to my peg. Because my peg for number four is a door, I might imagine a door made out of rulers. The more outrageous I can make my visual image, the easier it will be for me to remember. Therefore, I might imagine opening the door and having thousands of rulers falling on top of me.

When they are finished compiling the list, I give them the list forward or backward. Sometimes they call out random numbers and ask me for the item. I usually get applause for this "miracle." Then I share my peg system with them and give them a list to memorize in 10 minutes or less. Their responses are almost 100 percent accurate. From there we discuss how to use this strategy to study vocabulary by using definitions in their visual images. An example would be the word *pachyderm*. Its definition is "a thick-skinned animal." If it is the first word on the list (remembering that the peg for one is sun), the students may visualize an elephant in the hot sun sweating so much that his thick skin is falling off! In this way the word and the definition are attached to the peg. The students enjoy creating the "pictures" as they use this mnemonic device.

Acronyms are another mnemonic device. Acronyms are initials of the items you need to know put in a format that is easy to remember.

Vivid visual images are helpful when using a peg system.

Figure 6.3. A Rhyming Peg System	
Number 1	the sun
Number 2	my shoe
Number 3	a tree
Number 4	a door
Number 5	a hive
Number 6	a stick
Number 7	heaven
Number 8	a gate
Number 9	a line
Number 10	a hen

Acronyms and acrostics can help students learn certain facts.

R.O.Y. G. B.I.V. is one I recall from my childhood. It stood for the colors of the rainbow: red, orange, yellow, green, blue, indigo, and violet. Another acronym helped me remember the names of the Great Lakes: H.O.M.E.S. stood for Huron, Ontario, Michigan, Erie, and Superior.

Similar to an acronym is an acrostic—a memory device in which you make up a sentence using the first letter of each word or idea you want to remember. How about the musical staff—EGBDF? "Every good boy does fine" is the sentence I recall.

Give students the opportunity to create and share their own memory strategies.

Some of the best mnemonic devices are those that some of my students currently use. I have asked them to write down and share their learning techniques. This is a real eye-opener for some students. Most of them know nothing about mnemonic strategies, yet some successful learners have devised similar strategies that, when shared, can benefit everyone. Some students have been "chunking" information into small bits for many years. They then devise strategies that work with their individual learning styles. For instance, one student places his notes, divided into small chunks, at the end of his pool table. Taking one chunk at a time, he walks around the table and repeats the information until he knows it. Other students tried this, and some found it helpful.

Changing Lanes

Most semantic teaching strategies attempt to construct word and text information in a way that places it in other memory lanes as well as the semantic lane. Although many of us have been using these semantic techniques all along, we have been unaware of the lane shift taking place. The next chapter provides a closer view of the lanes less traveled, so we can use them to help our students learn.

Semantic teaching strategies allow word information to be processed and used in semantic and other memory lanes.

7

The Lanes Less Traveled: Instructional Strategies for Episodic, Procedural, Automatic, and Emotional Memory

A feeling of security is necessary for the brain to access information and form new memories.

It is easy to contaminate learning and confuse memory.

Throughout the school year my students work together on teams. I like this brain-compatible strategy because it helps in classroom management and bookkeeping and adds to students' feelings of security.

As I change units of study, I usually change teams. This provides variety for both the students and me. It also guards against the inevitable hierarchy that develops on all teams (Sylwester, 1997b). If a student feels uncomfortable about a position in the hierarchy, I try to keep that position as short-term and as painless as possible.

After a particularly tough nonfiction unit in literature, I decide the kids need a change, and I form new teams. They enjoy the teams so much that I decide to use these same teams in their language arts classes. The students do not object when they come to this class, and I assign teams to their new seating arrangements. We are studying indirect objects. I am trying to prepare them for a unit test, so I begin the class with a review. The sentences on the board are ready for the students to classify in our usual way. Many of my students look at the sentences on the board as though they were written in another language. They do not know how to classify the sentences. I am outraged! How could they have forgotten? Have they left their brains at home? We have been working on this idea for three days! What is wrong with these students?

The answer, of course, is nothing. It is my mistake. I have stripped my students of their episodic memory of the sentence patterns. Just by changing their placement in the classroom, I was preventing them from accessing certain memories.

I now had a choice. I could either move them back to their original seats or reteach them in their new ones. I chose to reteach the subject matter because I wanted to find out how much time the reteaching would take. It took three days before the students were back at their original skill levels.

The Paths of Least Resistance

Deliberate strategies can access the episodic, procedural, automatic, and emotional memory lanes. Using these strategies when planning a unit can make the information more enjoyable and easier to learn. Keeping in mind that all lanes should be accessed, let's go through each one separately.

Episodic Memory Strategies

Episodic memory is location driven. Studies have shown that if people receive information in a specific location they will more easily remember it in that same location. To use episodic memory effectively may take a little thought, energy, and some creativity.

Bulletin boards may be the easiest place to begin. For each unit covered, create a bulletin board that is unique enough to stand out from all of the others that you have used. Include pictures, posters, and symbols. Examples of how a problem or solution should look may impress your students. Even if you take the bulletin board down before a test, that information may still appear in your students' minds. Several weeks of looking at the board should leave an impression. Although the information becomes "invisible," the learning is stored in the episodic memory.

Changing the arrangement of the desks in your room, including your own, will help you and your students better use the episodic memory lane. Students who sit in the same spot week after week could begin to confuse information. In addition to changing the seating chart, change the arrangement of the students. Perhaps you can change the number of students on a team or put students in pairs. Change the desks or tables from rows to a circle or some other geometric shape. This will help make the material unique to the new look of your classroom.

Accessorize! Wear hats, scarves, belts, shoes, masks, or full costumes to enhance the learning experience. If you are studying the Civil War, find an old Yankee or Confederate cap to wear throughout the unit.

Moving students around strips them of their episodic memory.

Episodic memory is location driven.

Bulletin boards may be the easiest way to begin to create episodic memories.

Changing the arrangement of the classroom before each unit will help make the information unique.

Better yet, have each student make a hat to wear. This will make the information memorable and real.

Move out of your room. Perhaps you can use the library or go outside to learn some material. Take field trips. Anything you can do to make the learning unique may make the learning permanent. This may be possible for only very short units.

Use one color of paper for all the handouts related to a unit. This will help your students remember information that was on that color of paper. They will not need to recall anything on the reams of white paper they usually receive. In my English classes I prepare definition sheets using different colors for each unit. I simply remind my students to think about the "yellow" sheets or the "blue" sheets as I ask them to recall.

Teach from a specific area of the room. For each area of study change the location from which you teach. Recalling your location will help students recall the information more readily. They will associate your location with the information you shared.

Episodic memory techniques can do more than help students remember. They can also add to the enjoyment of learning. The brain likes novelty. It is intrigued by it, and it pays attention to it (Jensen, 1996). You will not be overstimulating your students with these changes. Instead, you'll be offering them a better opportunity to remember.

Procedural Memory Strategies

There are two ways to help students access their procedural memory lane. One is to have students perform the material often enough that it becomes a procedure. The other is to set up procedures in your classroom that will create strong memories. Let's look at each way.

When a procedure is repeated frequently, the brain stores it in the cerebellum for easy access. In the past, science was one of the only subject areas that was conducive to this way of storing information. Laboratory procedures were common, and these methods created strong learning experiences. Sometimes, however, even in the science lab, work is not repeated enough to become a procedure. Today, hands-on techniques can be used in many subject areas to provide procedural memories. Math students use manipulatives to develop their conceptual understanding and to solve problems. The problems change, but the procedure for doing them does not. With enough repetition, the students remember the procedure. English students use magnetized labels and follow a process to label each part of speech in a sentence on a magnetized board. Repetition allows them to store this process. This technique is not really any different from fire or earthquake drills. The purpose of such drills is to cement a safety procedure in children's brains—a procedure that may save lives.

Field trips add to learning and to episodic memory.

Teaching from a specific area of the room will help students use their episodic memories.

Setting up procedures in the classroom can help create strong memories.

Repetition of procedures is necessary to create a strong long-term memory pathway.

You—or your students—can also invent procedures, so that the students will, through repetition, place subject matter into procedural memory (Hannaford, 1995). Try anything that provides movement—for example, role-playing, debate, dance, marches, monologues, and games. Making shadow boxes can enhance procedural memory. Sock-puppet shows can reinforce many concepts in any content area. These procedures not only reinforce semantic knowledge, but they also represent memories that can be stored through those procedural memory "muscles." If you have trouble applying your content to any of these, use your imagination. Have students stand up as you cover specific material. Ask them to walk as you review it, jump when they think they understand a particular point, and clap when they know it all. All of that movement and fun will make a big impression on their brains.

Students can invent procedures to support instructional material.

Automatic Memory Strategies

The automatic memory lane stores multiplication tables, the alphabet, the ability to decode words, and dozens of other memories triggered by simple associations. Strategies for accessing this memory lane are simple and fun.

Anything that involves movement will enhance procedural memory.

The strategy I highly recommend is music. Putting information to music is simple for students of all ages. They usually find songs easy to remember, and they can then practice the information daily. For years I have had students learn the 48 prepositions, 23 helping verbs, and 18 linking verbs by writing their own songs. They use old, tried-and-true melodies, but they make up the lyrics. It can be as simple as taking "Mary Had a Little Lamb" and replacing all of the words with the list of words the students need to remember. Raps and poems can work as well. It becomes a reflex to fill in the newly learned words when the music begins (Jensen, 1998). I have had students return after high school and tell me they still know their songs.

Music is one of the most powerful means for enhancing automatic memory.

Other automatic strategies include the use of flash cards, repetition through daily oral work (in math, geography, language, vocabulary, and so on), and oral conditioning (for example, I say "Lincoln," you say "Gettysburg Address"). Each of these strategies has its own benefits. Students will tire of the same strategy, so provide variety. Quiz shows may be a great way to get responses to the automatic level; many students love this technique.

Emotional Memory Strategies

Without a doubt, emotional memory strategies are the most powerful. Many of these strategies also activate other memory storage areas that make them even more powerful. Both positive and negative emotions

Emotions activate many storage areas.

cause the brain to release certain neurotransmitters that aid in memory retention (LeDoux, 1996). That is not to say you should encourage negative emotions in your classroom, but simply to point out that strong feelings about content can add to emotional memory.

Music can be powerful in emotional memory. Using dramatic music as background while you read or discuss material can make the information meaningful. Playing the theme from "Mission Impossible" or "Dragnet" before you discuss the Battle of Gettysburg will get your students' attention and elicit feelings about the material.

Celebrations are emotional. These can be done with or without music. Plan special celebrations as students learn the material. Have the students present the material to the class through role-playing or a dramatic performance. Give them an emotion that they must try to convey and ask the class to try to recognize it. Find material that contradicts what is said in the text and that calls for debate. This technique can be very effective as students choose sides. Play devil's advocate and speak against the points you cover. Students love the opportunity to prove their teacher is wrong. Either way, it becomes an emotional experience.

Make your room the scene of the crime. If you are studying the Civil War, create the emotions felt in the era. Divide your room in half with a Mason-Dixon line. Separate the students and tell them what possessions they can keep. Allow the emotions to build as some lose their belongings and others receive them.

Most important of all is that you show your enthusiasm for your subject. Model your love of the content, and your students may find it contagious. If you share feelings about what you are teaching, your students may find that they can feel the same way about it.

Accessing Multiple Memory Lanes

The more memory lanes you can reach and teach to, the more successful your students will be in their learning. As this chapter indicates, some strategies can access more than one memory lane. This only makes your job easier. Like anything else dealing with brain-compatible learning, the more aware you are of this information, the easier it will be to use it on a conscious level.

Storytelling is a dynamic way of using multiple lanes. The brain processes parts and wholes simultaneously. Putting semantic information into a story format gives the students the whole idea and the details (Caine & Caine, 1994). Besides the semantic information, emotional memory can be tapped through the conflict or plot of the story. Episodic memory may be reached through the location in which you tell the story

Music can also be a powerful stimulus for emotional memory.

Debate and role-playing are effective ways to evoke emotions.

Your own enthusiasm for the subject matter may be contagious.

The more aware you are of information about brain-compatible strategies, the more likely you are to use it.

and how you dress.

As you plan a unit of instruction, evaluate how much of the material is aimed at the semantic lane. Are there ways you can teach that information through the other lanes? If not, review the semantic strategies described in the previous chapter and choose those that will work well with the content you are teaching.

Next decide how you can create an environment that will engage the episodic memory. What kind of bulletin boards and posters can you use? Do you need to make something? Better yet, can your students make the items to decorate for this "episode"? Are there things that you can wear that will enhance learning? Will your students be able to bring, carry, or wear anything that will make this experience more memorable?

Analyze the material to determine which procedures are built in or which ones you can create. Will the students learn better standing, sitting, or moving in some way? Are there manipulatives for this unit? Can you or your students create a dance or ritual to accompany the learning? One procedure that combines episodic memory with procedural involves making a bulletin board and decorations, and then having the students put them up. This will add information to both lanes.

Think about how you can make some learning automatic. Are flash cards a possibility? What information can be put to music? Repetition is a plus; try to find a way to use it.

Can you make this material emotional? Are there popular songs that might be associated with this material? Ask the students what they know about this new information. This may add to their feelings about it. How will you celebrate the beginning of the unit? How will you celebrate the end? What kind of role-playing or debates can you use to elicit strong feelings?

A novel that I sometimes read with my class is *The Rifle* by Gary Paulsen. This incredible book covers the "life" of a rifle from its creation to the present. The technical parts are difficult to follow; yet those sections are surrounded by a moving story of life and death. When I use this powerful book, I engage my students in the entire production of the unit.

I begin by asking them how they feel about guns and gun control. The answers vary among students, some of whom are beginning to hunt with their fathers. The emotional responses that I receive are steps in the right direction. We discuss drive-by shootings, hijackings, skyjackings, and the latest mass murders at schools. The students are ready to do battle over the issue. I ask the students to bring in any newspaper or magazine clippings that deal with guns. I also ask for

---

Look at the semantic information in the curriculum and try to find ways to present it through the episodic, automatic, procedural, and emotional memory lanes.

Begin with the episodic lane and continue with the procedural lane.

Celebrate both the beginning and the end of a unit to add to emotional memory.

Ask the students how they feel about the topic to be studied.

Have students decorate the classroom to add to their procedural and episodic memories.

Offer students choices in their learning.

Research procedures may access multiple memory lanes.

Daily repetition of important information is a key to building long-term memory.

pictures of guns.

The students bring in the needed materials to decorate the room. As they enter, I have the song "I Fought the Law, and the Law Won" playing on the boom box. The students smile or chuckle as they listen to the song. They share their information or pictures. Then they place the items around the room. By the end of the class period, the room is decorated, and the students have a basic knowledge of gun control and legislation in the United States. They have also heard some horror stories about accidental deaths and rampages by people with guns.

The next day the students choose a slip of paper from one of two piles. Half the slips say "Guns kill people." The other half say "People kill people." The students who choose "Guns kill people" sit on one side of the room. The others take the other side. I hand out the novels, and the reading begins.

So far the episodic, procedural, and emotional lanes have been activated. Playing the song each day as the students enter will trigger memories of this information.

As we read, we encounter the technical information and terms involved in building a rifle. To make this more meaningful for the students, I must discover a way for them to understand the process. We cannot build a gun ourselves because weapons or replicas are not allowed in school. We can draw. I provide paper, dictionaries, and encyclopedias. Informative Web sites on the Internet can be helpful here, too. As the novel describes the building of the rifle, we draw our own pictures in stages. We talk about the procedures used, laugh about some of them, and act out a few.

As the reading continues, we discover that the rifle passes through the hands of many people in the story. We begin to create a story map on the board. Each section has a picture of the new owner, along with a description of the person and an explanation of how he received the rifle.

Some days I ask students to come to the front of the room. I give each of them a sign to wear with the name of one of the rifle owners or another character in the story. The students discuss the order in which the owners should stand, and then one or several students retell the story. They pass a picture of the rifle from owner to owner. Other days I hand the picture to a student and say, "You are the builder of the rifle. Who are you?" Then the student gives the rifle to another student and says, "I sold the rifle to you. Who are you?" This continues until we come to the current owner. I give written quizzes occasionally to test the learning.

By now I have activated emotional, procedural, episodic, and semantic memories. With repetition of things like the names of the owners of the guns, students have some information in automatic memory.

At this point, I ask the students to create a song about the story. They can use the tune from "I Fought the Law" or compose one of their own. I assign this to each group, so that we will have only two songs when we finish. The songs should be very different, and they are. The students begin to sing their songs each day after class begins. The songs are full of information from the story.

Creating songs with unit content accesses both automatic and emotional lanes.

When we reach the end of the story, most students are very emotional about the events leading up to the ending and the ending itself. Again, we have reached a technical area of the story. I need a way to help them understand. We reenact the scene. Students volunteer to be characters from the story. We create signs with names on them. One student becomes the rifle itself, and another becomes the bullet. The rifle shoots, and the bullet follows the path described in the book. The role-play is not perfect, but it appears to work. Many students are fascinated by the physics involved in the bullet's path.

Use student volunteers to reenact or reteach the information.

As the unit culminates, I ask the students if they are still comfortable in their chosen groups. Many stay where they are. Some switch sides. They ask for debates. They spend the next several days preparing. We hold the debates, and the students discover the importance of preparation and evidence.

Debates may cement semantic information through the emotional and procedural lanes.

The final activity is a persuasive essay using the group titles as the argument. The unit ends. The students return to their previous seats. The posters, pictures, and articles are returned. Most students appear to have enjoyed the experience.

I had to use conscious effort to access all of those memory lanes. The unit became more interesting as I did so. The students were involved and happy. Each year I must add some units and change others to access all of the memory lanes. It can be a challenge, but the rewards are worth it.

You may find that your work becomes more interesting as you make the effort to access and create more memories for your students.

Many of you have been creating units for years that access the various memory lanes. Brain research encourages us to enrich our teaching strategies. Knowing this information may enlarge your bank of teaching strategies. Use the strategies that fit your style.

When I started teaching in 1971, I didn't have a style. Even though I had fun teaching and my students were learning, I did not have a clue about what I should be doing. Through the years I have taken classes, attended workshops, and read hundreds of books as I searched for a style that would fit me. It took a long time to find a style that allowed me to feel satisfied that I was doing the job I wanted to do. There are days when I

Brain research reinforces most of our best teaching strategies.

want to tear my hair out and throw in the towel. When I give myself the chance to step back and look at what I am doing, I usually see that I have slipped back into my old patterns—you know, the ones that I used repeatedly and expected different results from. I find that when I return to my brain-compatible methods, both my students and I feel successful.

8

Producing the Evidence: Assessment That Mirrors Instructional Strategies

I love teaching Greek mythology. It is one of my favorite units. I fell in love with the genre in high school, and I have collected paraphernalia and added to the unit since 1971. Through the years, because of my training in brain-compatible teaching and learning, I have changed the unit and made it more brain-friendly. Or so I thought.

Just a few years ago I made some big mistakes. The unit was great. I divided the kids into teams named for the gods and goddesses. They thought it was cool. They had to read myths, do some fun activities, and produce a final product of their choice. The students presented fabulous puppet shows, made interesting newspapers, acted out scenes from their favorite myths, created posters, and did radio and television interviews. They made advertisements for Greek products like "Medusa's Favorite Make-up: It may cake a little, but it won't crumble!"

I had a great time teaching the material. The students had a great time learning and producing—at least, I thought they were learning. At the end of the unit, I did what most of us do. I gave the students a written assessment, containing only the material we had covered. I took the test before I gave it to them to be sure it was fair.

The results were embarrassing. The grades were horrendous. I was very angry with my students. Why hadn't they studied? Did they think this was all fun and games? Was it possible that I had failed? Then it finally occurred to me. I couldn't blame the kids, their parents, or even the full moon. I had taught them through various memory lanes, and I had assessed them through only one. The one I chose was the one I had used and reinforced the least.

> We have all taught units that we thought were wonderful and then have been disappointed with the results.

> Retrieved memories are the only evidence we have of learning.

Assessments That Work

Some interpreters of brain research will suggest that you give up traditional testing because it can be antagonistic to the brain (Jensen, 1995). I do not disagree with them; however, as a classroom teacher who has taught in many traditional districts, I understand how necessary traditional testing can be. Perhaps because of my college training or because of my need for "concrete" information, I often find it necessary to give traditional assessments to my students. I have the assessments available to show to parents, and I can explain them easily. I have the information if there is a question about grades. Even with the new rubrics for more "authentic assessment," many parents don't understand or relate to this approach. Therefore, I often end my units with a traditional assessment aimed specifically at the semantic memory lane.

Students have been trained or have trained themselves to study for these traditional tests. These are the kids who are always asking, "Do we have to know this?" or "Will this be on the test?" I sometimes want to scream when they ask such questions, but I know that they have every right to ask them.

We would like to think that our students have a love of learning. Many of them do. However, most educational systems are set up so that the bottom line—grades—is the most important component. I believe that our students do love learning. Those dendrites are always looking for information. However, that information may not be the kind that comes straight out of a book.

The question remains: *How do we teach and assess our students in a natural, enjoyable, brain-compatible way and still get the results and the data that we need to give to our districts, our administrators, and our parents?*

Portfolio Assessment

One nontraditional, brain-compatible form of assessment is a student portfolio. A portfolio is a collection of work that shows growth over time or samples of students' best work. It may include journals, essays, letters, tests, worksheets, audiotapes, videotapes, posters, and any other work samples.

Working portfolios may give both the student and the teacher a clearer idea of how the student is progressing. It may be easier to perceive evidence of a student's ability to apply concepts through portfolio work samples than through traditional assessments.

Suzanne is not a very good math student. Her scores reveal that. Her most recent score on a test asking for solutions to problems using addition and subtraction was 65 percent.

Traditional testing is often necessary and in some cases desirable.

Parents often understand traditional assessment better than authentic assessment.

We like to think that our students have a love of learning.

How do we teach and assess in a brain-compatible manner and still get the results we need?

Portfolios are brain compatible and provide a great deal of information about student progress.

Sarah, on the other hand, shines in math class. She has almost perfect 100s in the grade book. She raises her hand in class constantly. She makes the teacher, her mother, and herself very happy.

Which child knows more about math? At first glance, one would assume that Sarah does because of her test scores. However, further inspection reveals some interesting information. In her portfolio, Suzanne keeps a "collection book" for her weekly paper route. It is her responsibility to collect money from her customers each month. Suzanne's book is well organized and precise. She has a separate page for each customer showing the amount paid, the amount owed, and a balance for each month. Does Suzanne know math?

Portfolios are one way of bringing the real world into the classroom. Students can reveal a great deal about themselves by what they choose to keep in their portfolios. Many enjoy bringing items from home. This may convey the feeling that the portfolio really belongs to them. On occasion the students inspect and reflect on their portfolio items.

Discovering a child's true interests and abilities may be possible only through portfolios.

Performance Assessment

Other nontraditional assessments are often called *performance assessments*. This rather broad term describes any assessment in which the student may demonstrate knowledge and understanding through various means. Giving students a choice of assessments is a brain-compatible approach that allows students to access the information through the memory lane of their choice.

Authentic assessment is a performance assessment in which a student demonstrates mastery of a task that is considered "real life." Many educators use this type of assessment. The drawback is the time required.

Performance assessments are an important component of assessment that honors the uniqueness of students' brains. Appropriate rubrics enable this kind of assessment to be objective.

Performance assessments allow students to demonstrate their knowledge and understanding through various means.

Life in the Fast Lanes:
Matching Assessments to the Memory Lanes

Let's look at each memory lane and good methods of assessment for each. Remember, retrieved memories are the only proof we have that learning has taken place. Students need to be able to show us what they know. If they have learned information and stored it through multiple memory lanes, appropriate assessment strategies will help them retrieve those memories.

Matching assessments to the memory lanes is easy.

Episodic Memory Assessment

Can you assess students through the episodic memory lane? We do it all the time. Except for most standardized testing, most of us do our assessments in the room in which we taught the material. It can be as simple as that.

Studies have shown that people who are taught information in one place access it more easily in the same place. A study conducted underwater proves the point. Subjects who were given information while diving remembered that information more readily when they were in the water rather than on dry land (Baddeley, 1990).

If you have consciously created a context for learning by using some of the suggestions in the preceding chapter, your students should be able to access the episodic memory lane for any type of assessment in that location. You can test this by removing your bulletin board materials and asking your students about the information that was there. Most will stare at the empty space left on the board and visualize the data. If you wore a hat or costume while teaching, wear it on the day of the assessment.

Remember that you are also covered with invisible information. Your presence in the room will make a difference. I spent years being angry with math teachers. When my students had to figure grades on papers, they could never multiply with fractions or decimals. I assumed those teachers weren't doing their jobs. I now know that the students were lacking the episodic memory connections to math. They could do the work in their math rooms or with their math teachers present. Invisible information is powerful. Therefore, do not have your substitute teacher give an exam.

Yes, I have often heard the argument that we are not doing our children justice by letting them rely on episodic memory. They should be able to apply the information in the real world wherever they go. This argument has strong points. However, I ask myself, "How real-world is the world of education?" How often in the real world are we given the kinds of assessments that we give in school? Education is moving closer and closer to real-world situations and authentic types of assessment. Meanwhile, we must do the best we can with what we have.

Assessment is stressful for all of us. How many of us are relaxed and happy when our evaluation time comes? We may enjoy sharing and showing what we can do, but when it comes time for the verbal and written evaluations, most of us get quite nervous. So do our students. I believe that any advantage I can give my students for receiving and retrieving information will ultimately benefit them wherever they go.

Each memory lane has a compatible method of assessment.

Studies have shown that people who are taught information in one location will access it more easily in the same location.

Your presence in the room during assessment will affect your students' performance.

How often in the real world are we given the types of assessments that we give our students?

Procedural Memory Assessment

This is the "how to" lane. These memories are difficult for any of us to convey through words alone. If you do not believe me, try to do one of the following. Without using your hands, explain to someone how to tie shoes, how to apply eye make-up, or how to play the baby game "Pat-a cake." Difficult to do? Of course. The reason is that these are procedures that you have learned through movement, and the best way to retrieve those memories is through those same movements. Yet we constantly ask our students to share information with paper and pencil.

The simple solution is to have students show you the procedure. You may say that this is not so simple because you have 25 to 30 students in your classroom, or you may teach six classes per day for only 45 minutes. How can you assess all of those students doing a procedure that takes several minutes? Here are some solutions.

If the assessment is on science lab work, take the students into the lab. Allow their episodic memories to work. Give them the equipment used for the procedure if it is available. Either with or without the actual chemicals or other substances, allow them to "walk" through the process, writing down each step as they work. Once they have done this, they can answer some application, analysis, and synthesis questions on a traditional assessment.

Another method is to put them in the small groups they worked with and have the groups show you the procedure. If they understand the procedure, you will see that they have difficulty not doing the steps assigned to the other members of their group. Ask each student specific questions during the demonstration. Use a rubric to evaluate each student's performance. Again, after the procedure, you may want to give them questions of application, analysis, and synthesis. Perhaps you will want to give them another problem to solve using the same procedure but changing group members' roles. Keep a log of the class or use a section of your grade book to record the progress of each student.

Once the brain stores information in procedural memory, that information is easy to retrieve given the appropriate opportunity. Allow for those opportunities in your classroom whenever possible.

Automatic Memory Assessment

Automatic memory retrieval is similar to procedural memory retrieval. I think of the information stored in the cerebellum as long strings of neurons hooked together by strong and healthy dendrites and axons. They appear like dominoes. All I have to do is trigger the first neuron, and they fire in a systematic way, just as the fall of the first domino triggers the others to fall in turn.

A procedural memory is difficult to convey through words alone.

Allow students to walk through a procedure to trigger memory.

Anything learned through movement is best assessed through that same movement.

Ask students specific questions while they are doing the procedure.

Information stored in automatic memory must be accessed in the same manner in which it was taught.

For this type of memory retrieval, I simply have the students give me the information orally or have them write it down. For instance, if it is in a song, they either sing it with their groups (I never make them sing alone), or they can sing it to themselves as they write it on paper. If I want to assess their application of the material, I ask them to write the automatic information on their papers first. Then they can refer to it as they apply.

> The students finally have their linking-verb songs memorized. They sing them willingly, and I am pleased with the results. They have taken an oral quiz by standing in front of the room and singing with their groups. I watch their lips carefully and listen for each voice. I have also given them a written quiz. They had to write down the words on paper.
>
> We are beginning to classify sentences with linking verbs. The connection is not there! I find that many students who received As on their quizzes are puzzled and hesitant when they encounter a linking verb in a sentence! Are their automatic memories failing them?

My students were not making the connections that I hoped they would. I needed to include another step in this process. Once the information was in automatic memory, the students needed to practice using this skill with an application process. First they needed to write down from memory the linking verbs. Then they could proceed to the sentences, checking for those linking verbs. I assumed they would "automatically" do this. Some of them could, but many could not.

Emotional Memory Assessment

Accessing students' feelings during the teaching process is far easier than during the assessment process. Emotional memories are powerful enough to override logical thinking. Sticking to the facts may be difficult depending on how emotional the issues have become. In dealing with the rifle story described in chapter 7, students sometimes allowed their feelings and opinions to overwhelm them, and they retrieved very little factual information.

Most emotional memories are not so overpowering. When emotions are involved, some students can retrieve them through performance. A project such as role-playing, a puppet show, or a skit would be appropriate. Applying these emotional memory concepts to a different context may be beneficial as well. For instance, if you have studied a survival issue, rather than have the students reenact the survival situation you studied, have them create a new situation and apply the survival principles to it. Other students will need to apply and demonstrate their emotional memory

---

If you used music to activate automatic memory, assess your students using that music.

Give students the opportunity to make the connections between information stored in automatic memory and its use on a test.

Accessing emotional memory during the assessment process may be difficult.

Some students can access emotional memories through performance.

through written work. Writing newspaper articles, editorials, essays, or short stories, and creating posters are examples of this kind of emotional memory performance. What if you helped your students store information in emotional memory through celebration or music? Repeating that celebration and playing that music during a test will help them remember.

Perhaps you reached their emotions through your own enthusiasm. If this was one of your techniques, be enthusiastic on the day of the assessment. Try to get them as excited about what they have learned as you are. Explain to them that a test day is a day to share and celebrate what they have learned. Some teachers play special celebration music on the days of their exams.

If you have accessed the emotions of your students in your teaching, you have given them an incredible tool. Emotions will take priority over everything else in the brain. Assessing students through their emotional memories will also be an opportunity for you to assess emotional intelligence (Goleman, 1995). Do your students understand their feelings about the topic? Have their feelings changed in any way? Do they understand the feelings of others? Have they displayed empathy? Assessing emotional intelligence is sometimes tricky, yet giving your students the opportunity to consider these key issues may be the most important learning of all. Keeping a journal would be a wonderful way for them to self-assess.

Semantic Memory Assessment

You may be thinking that this section is unnecessary because you have been giving tests for years. But you need to be aware of this: if information is stored in the semantic lane, then giving traditional tests usually works; if the information has not been stored there, your students will underperform. Aren't there always a few students in your room who consistently underperform on the tests, yet you are certain that they were "getting it" when you were teaching?

In chapter 4 I talked about looking in the bakery aisle for the milk. Perhaps your students are looking in the semantic lane and not retrieving information because it's not there. This brings us to two questions. Do you feel the need to give traditional semantic assessments? If so, can you take memories from another lane and somehow get them into the semantic lane for this type of test?

For me the answer to both questions is yes. I want to give traditional paper-and-pencil tests. Why? I believe in balance. I use both authentic and traditional assessment with most units because I feel students need to learn to handle both types. Also, I want to meet the needs of the students who feel safe and secure with traditional tests. They do well on these, and I want them to feel successful.

Display the same enthusiasm when you assess as you did when you taught the material.

Keeping a journal can be a wonderful way for students to self-assess.

Can you take information from another lane and get it into the semantic lane?

Traditional tests have a place in the brain-compatible classroom.

Changing Lanes: Teach to the Test!

So here's the good news: We can retrieve memories from other lanes and put them in the semantic lane. One method involves doing what you have repeatedly been told not to do: Teach to the test. Begin by working backwards. What do you expect your students to gain from the material you are covering? Be sure you cover those points. Then give practice tests. Yes, this takes time; but in the end you and your students will be happier. In other words, you must give your students the opportunity to practice taking information from one of the other lanes and using it semantically, with words. As you give the practice tests, talk the students through it. Remind them of the procedures, the automatic memories they have, the emotional content, and have them look around the room at the episodic information. If you played music during the learning activities, play the music at least during the practice tests. All of this will allow your students to change lanes or access all of them. (Had I done this during the Greek mythology unit, it would have made a great difference in the results.)

If you used any of the semantic strategies from chapter 6, allow your students to use these on the assessment. For example, many teachers who use the power-picture or mind-map technique ask their students to recreate the picture or map from memory and put it on the back of the exam. Because the main purpose of this technique is to build visual memory, the students will probably be able to do this. Then allow them to use that information to help them answer the test questions. Some teachers give extra credit for the map. The important point is that you taught your students a strategy and now you are showing them how to apply it.

This approach will work with other semantic techniques. If your students used a peg system, give them the opportunity to re-create it on their test paper. They can also re-create time lines, write down their acrostics or acronyms, or make an outline. Encourage them to put the techniques they have learned to good use. This will be a lesson in how to transfer information.

The students should have information stored by means of the other semantic techniques that you used, such as role-playing and peer teaching, in their semantic lanes. Retrieving most of that information should be easy.

You can use any of the semantic techniques suggested for retrieving information from multiple lanes. That is the beauty of many of these techniques. The peg system takes semantic information and places it in automatic memory. The power-picture technique takes semantic information and places it in the procedural and usually the emotional lanes because the students often become emotionally attached to their drawings.

Semantic tests will provide true accountability only if information was taught to that lane.

Practice tests are a practical way to begin to move information from any other memory lane into the semantic lane.

Students can re-create power pictures or other visual organizers as part of the assessment.

Encourage students to put the techniques they have learned to good use.

If you had the students work with others creating any of these mnemonic devices, emotions were probably involved. Any technique involving students working together may have led to emotional memory storage.

Designing Tests for Memory Retrieval

You can use a traditional paper-and-pencil test to access different memory lanes. This may take a little extra time; however, you may be able to change your current tests very easily. The following examples provide ideas for targeting each memory lane.

- *Automatic Memory.* Use sentence completion. The associations that your students have made are readily available with this technique.
  Example: The rifle was first given to _____.
- *Emotional Memory.* Use "feeling" words.
  Example: The creator of the rifle was sad to lose it because _____.

or

Why was the creator of the rifle sad about losing it?
- *Procedural Memory.* Use transition words that will help the student remember the procedure.
  Example: After the water is heated, you should _____.

or

Between heating the water and adding sodium, which of the following should be done?
(a) add calcium
(b) turn off the burner
(c) cool the water down
(d) turn off the lights
- *Episodic Memory.* Refer to locational materials in your questions.
  Example: According to the information on the periodic table, the abbreviation for iron is _____.
- *Semantic Memory.* Allow the students to re-create mnemonic devices.
  Example: On the back of the paper write your peg system for the list of the presidents.

or

Remind them of the other strategies.
Example: When we role-played the Battle of Gettysburg, the battle was won by _____.

Any technique involving students working together may tap into emotional memory storage.

"Feeling" words on traditional tests may trigger emotional memories.

Allow students to re-create mnemonic devices.

The Strategies in Action

In an effort to share memory strategies with my students, I often create situations that clearly show them how the different memory lanes work. This reinforces for both them and me the awareness that memories can be consciously made more powerful. The following activity was described in the book *Memory* by Margulies and Sylwester (1998):

> It is Brain Awareness Week. I am spending the entire week sharing information with my students about the brain and learning. After several days of discussion and demonstrations on the structure and the function of the brain, we are ready to move on to short-term and long-term memory.
>
> I have planned an interesting experiment to try with my students. I divide the class in half. I send one group to the library to memorize a long list of facts. They may use any method they choose, and they may work alone or as a group. These students willingly leave. The remaining group listens to a story. The story is on tape and includes music. All of the facts that the other group is memorizing are presented within the context of the story.
>
> When the story concludes after about 20 minutes, I bring both groups together. I question the groups orally. Group members may work together to confer on answers. I am eager to discover if the listeners will do better because they formed more emotional memories. I know that information in this format is generally recalled easily. I also want to determine whether the memorizers will excel because they used good strategies.
>
> We investigate the results. Both groups do well. Why? My students give me the answer during our discussion of the process. The listeners believe they missed out by not having a visual to follow. A few of them took notes, but not many. The memorizers agree completely. They found that through working together and seeing the list, memorizing it was easy. They had fun working together, so they also had an emotional component.

Let's examine the techniques used and the memories stored by each group:

- The *listeners* had music with lyrics played repeatedly to help the automatic memory, emotional content in the story to help the emotional lane, and semantic information in story form to help the episodic memory. The listeners also had the advantage of learning and being tested in

Discuss the memory lanes with your students, so they understand how they learn.

Students need to experience how the memory lanes can work for them.

Most students find that working together facilitates learning.

Music and the ability to move around help many students access memories.

the same room.

• The *memorizers* had a visual list of semantic information, the opportunity to talk to each other and listen (semantic memory), and the ability to move around while learning (procedural memory). In addition, they shared semantic strategies that each used, and they had fun working together (emotional memory).

Both groups earned similar scores on tests given immediately after the learning experience and a week later. However, on an individual performance test given three weeks later, each of the listeners answered at least two more questions correctly than did the memorizers.

Based on this classroom research, I concluded that a story format may be beneficial for long-term memory. I discussed with my students the possibilities of yet another strategy—taking the semantic information from their textbooks and making a story out of it. Although they felt this might be a tedious task, many thought writing the story would be an enjoyable group project.

Putting information into story format usually allows the information to travel along different lanes.

Test Anxiety

Keep in mind that many of your students suffer from test anxiety. This is a physical problem that triggers the stress response. Many students are not so stressed that they can't use their memory lanes. However, for some students, this can be a major difficulty.

Test anxiety is a common problem.

Many students will have an easier time retrieving information through different lanes, and this is information you should share with them. Try to encourage them by saying you will be approaching the unit in a way that will make it easier for them to learn and remember. Knowing that you care can give students a sense of security that may prevent a stress response.

Pretesting, practice testing, and even retesting are sometimes appropriate and necessary. Our goal is to help students understand how they learn so they can be better learners. Some students believe they have poor memories. Many adults believe the same thing. What may actually be happening is that the memory is there, but the person is simply not accessing the appropriate memory lane. For our students, proof of their good memories becomes a grade. Grades are determined by assessments. We must offer students the opportunity to discover the power of their good memories and their wonderful brains.

For many students, proof of their good memories becomes a grade.

It is a particularly bad day. I feel as though I have no control in my classroom. The quiz I give is a disaster. It feels like I am working outside in

On some days, nothing seems to work.

the sun; I am hot and sticky. Why in the world am I working this hard under these conditions? I'm an intelligent person. I could probably get a job in an air-conditioned office and not have to talk to another child for months!

I bolt for the front door of the building and head for home. I grab the mail as I walk in my front door. All I want to do is rip off my clothes, jump in the shower, and then watch "Oprah." The stack of bills does not help my disposition, but beneath the requests for my hard-earned money is a letter from a former student. She writes that she has received a scholarship to a Midwestern university where she is studying to become a teacher. She says it is because I inspired her. She remembers the quotes I had hanging in my room, the preposition songs, the teamwork, and the fun we had. She says that her old classmates know that she is going to be a teacher "like Mrs. Sprenger."

Other days make all of the work worthwhile.

Well, that does it! The tears start to fall. I am not sure I cry because I am touched by these words or just because I deserve to cry today. The letter is written on notebook paper, and I take care not to tear it or soak it with tears. I walk to my box of laminating paper. I carefully laminate this letter that contains the words that will get me to school tomorrow morning.

9

Frequently Asked Questions

I am grateful that through the years the information I have shared seems to have made a difference in the outlooks and the lives of many educators and parents. It has been heartwarming to hear teachers say that because of the current research and related strategies they no longer count the days to retirement. They feel energized and loaded with ammunition for another school year.

Despite what we know about brain-compatible instruction, many questions remain unanswered simply because this is a new and emerging field of research. But there are some questions that educators consistently ask because we all share a love of children and a desire to do what is best for them. This chapter provides answers to some of those questions.

Although many questions about the brain remain unanswered, research has provided answers to others.

Question: *What are "windows of opportunity" in the brain? I have read about them, and I'm concerned that we are missing opportunities.*

The phrase *windows of opportunity* describes the periods available for development of specialized areas of the brain. These windows are also called *critical periods*. For example, the window of opportunity for vision does not close until age 10. Research is discovering that the human brain at birth is wired in an interconnected way (Neville, 1997). The areas of the newborn brain are not as differentiated as they are in the adult brain. Therefore, if neurons that are available for a distinct purpose are not used for that purpose by a specific developmental time, they will be adopted elsewhere. This means that a child whose eyes are covered during the early years may lose those visual neurons to the auditory area.

These windows of opportunity present themselves in other areas. The window for language development seems to be open from birth until about age 10. Many researchers believe that this is the time to teach foreign languages because neurons are available for different sounds. If a child does not hear the sounds by age 10, those neurons may not be

The areas of a newborn's brain are not as differentiated as the areas of an adult's brain.

"Windows of opportunity" in the brain are periods of time available for development of specialized brain areas.

Emotional development occurs in the first few years of life.

available again. Therefore, adults who learn a second language will usually have an accent that a child may not have. The first few years of life are critical for emotional development. If children are not nurtured, their brains are greatly affected, and they may never recover. In studies of neglected children in Rumanian orphanages, positron emission tomography (PET) scans show that their brains are underdeveloped in the emotional areas (Begley, 1997).

Researchers agree that the enormous amount of growth in the brain that begins during fetal development starts to end at about age 10. At this time, the brain is rapidly pruning unused synapses (Diamond & Hopson, 1998). This is not to say that the brain has difficulty learning from this point. It still rapidly learns and retains information. This pruning of synapses is simply the brain's way of disposing of what it perceives as unnecessary and abandoned connections. It's therefore easier for the brain to care for the important connections already made (Nash, 1997).

Question: *How can I keep my students' attention?*

Current research suggests that constant attention is not only impossible, but also undesirable. The brain needs time for both focusing and processing. Your students must first pay attention to the information being learned or discovered. Then they need time to make those connections in their brains—to form those neural networks that lead to long-term memory.

Prolonged attention to a learning experience may not be desirable.

Getting a student's attention is usually not a problem. There are many ways to attract attention. Emotional stimulus, novelty, movement, and music are a few. What most teachers are truly asking is, "Once I have their attention, how do I keep it?" This question deals directly with how long a student can focus.

Children of different ages can focus for different amounts of time. Research indicates that most children can focus for a number of minutes equal to their age plus two (Jensen, 1995). Therefore, a 6-year-old can focus for about eight minutes. After this focus time, the brain needs some time to process the information in a different way.

The number of minutes a student can focus is equal to the student's age plus two.

Ideally we should confine learning activities within those focus minutes and then allow for some movement to redirect the students' attention so that processing can take place. This is a time to try some of the semantic strategies previously mentioned, such as peer teaching or mind mapping.

Adults are not much different from children. They cannot focus for more than 15 to 20 minutes. I have found in my graduate classes that students need to take breaks, change activities, or engage in physical movement.

Many factors affect attention, such as diet, emotions, and hormones. We must encourage our students to eat in a brain-compatible way. This includes eating plenty of protein and drinking lots of fluids, and avoiding carbohydrates in large quantities (Jensen, 1998). Protein will help the brain stay alert by providing the amino acids to produce the alertness neurotransmitters dopamine and norepinephrine. The brain consists of about 80 percent water. Fluids are necessary to keep those connections strong. Excessive carbohydrates are calming. Limiting them helps keep an alert state (Wurtman, 1986).

Information enters our brain through our senses. A multisensory experience will provide a better opportunity for attention. Different brains favor different sensory stimulation. Kinesthetic learners need more movement, auditory learners need to talk about the material, and visual learners need to see something concrete. Appropriate teaching styles will allow each of those kinds of learners to lock in on the learning (Rose & Nicholl, 1997).

Emotional stimulus and novelty are the two biggest attention-getters. It helps to keep these in mind when planning lessons. Another factor is biological. Our biochemistry runs in 90-minute cycles that fluctuate throughout the day. More attentional neurotransmitters are available to us in the morning than in the afternoon (Sylwester, 1995). Perhaps that is why most primary teachers teach more difficult content in the morning and allow for more social interaction in the afternoon. This information should be a wake-up call for middle and secondary schools. Rotating schedules may be the most brain-compatible approach, allowing for periodic teaching of difficult content in the morning. One school at which I taught used such a schedule. It took teachers a while to adjust, but the kids loved it. All of us appreciated the variety, and the students who usually attended difficult content classes in the late afternoon had the opportunity to be more alert and receptive when class was held in the morning.

Another consideration is the brain's ability to pay attention. Research has found that the brain can direct its attention and block out another stimulus. In other words, if we direct our students to pay attention, they have more ability to do so. When we tell a student to "watch this carefully," a structure in the brain helps block out other stimuli and aids the occipital area in its focus. Norepinephrine may act to reduce background activity; less background electrical activity is present; and more blood flows to the areas of the brain that are focusing on the stimulus (Posner & Raichle, 1997).

Question: *What is going on in the mind of my 13-year-old? I just do not understand her!*

Many factors affect attention, such as diet, emotions, and hormones.

Information enters the brain through the senses.

Emotional stimulation and novelty are two big attention-getters.

The brain can direct its attention.

The mind of a 13-year-old can be puzzling.

Growth spurts occur in the brain at ages 10 to 12, 14 to 16, and 18 to 20.

This is a frequently asked question, though the specific age may vary somewhat. Adolescents' brains are enigmas for many. Researchers have generally found that growth spurts occur in the brain at ages 10 to 12, 14 to 16, and 18 to 20 (Diamond & Hopson, 1998). Brain growth plateaus between these periods of growth. Couple this with raging hormones and the result is a person who is difficult to understand. The adolescent is facing physical and emotional changes as adulthood approaches.

From the scientific perspective, brain growth at this stage is not comparable to brain growth during fetal development and the early years. Studies do show, however, that academic enrichment during the teenage years is very important. Because the brain is still pruning unnecessary synapses, we must provide stimulation to this maturing brain.

Academic enrichment during the teenage years is very important.

Teenagers need support. They want to fit in and be accepted in their newly developed bodies. From their perspective, belonging and fitting in is more important than schoolwork. This need to belong may stem from the human brain's adaptation to life hundreds of years ago, when group interaction made survival possible. Teenagers need opportunities for groupwork and social interaction in their learning.

Question: *What is a really good brain diet?*

Certain foods cause the release of certain neurotransmitters.

To work well, your brain needs several readily available neurotransmitters. Acetylcholine is made from choline, which occurs in eggs, liver, and soy products. This chemical helps build long-term memory, so it is quite important. Norepinephrine and dopamine, sometimes called the alertness chemicals, are produced when tyrosine reaches the brain. Tyrosine is found in protein. Carbohydrates are also necessary for a healthy brain. Carbohydrates contain tryptophan, which causes the release of serotonin. Serotonin has a calming effect on the brain and body (Wurtman & Suffes, 1996). A substance called calpain cleans neurons' receptor sites. It is derived from calcium, and so the consumption of calcium aids memory (Howard, 1994).

Tyrosine, found in protein, produces the alertness chemicals.

If you have to be alert for most of the day, it makes sense to start the day with three or four ounces of protein. You may eat small amounts of carbohydrates with your meal. The tyrosine will reach your brain before the tryptophan and will prevent the release of serotonin. A protein-rich lunch will continue to keep you "on your toes" for the afternoon. Save most of your carbohydrates for late afternoon or for your evening meal. This is a time when you will probably be more able and willing to relax.

Drink water. The brain consists of about 78 percent water, and it needs to be kept hydrated (Jensen, 1998).

Question: *What is the difference between a CAT scan, a PET scan, and an MRI?*

Each of these is an imaging technique that is currently used to study the brain. *CT* or *CAT* stands for "computed tomography," a type of study that uses radiation to produce images of slices of the brain. This shows the density of the tissue.

MRI and *functional MRI* refer to "magnetic resonance imaging." These images show great detail without using radiation. By using a large magnetic field, the atoms in the brain are mapped. The MRI images the structure of the brain, and the functional MRI images both structure and function. As the patient performs mental or physical tasks, the amount of oxygen consumed in the blood in certain parts of the brain can be measured.

A *PET* scan refers to "positron emission tomography." This procedure also looks at a slice of the brain. The patient is injected with radioactive glucose and asked to perform a task. The glucose will be concentrated in the areas of the brain that are being used. High levels of the radioactive glucose show which areas of the brain are functioning for particular mental and physical tasks (Cohen, 1996).

Imaging techniques, such as positron emission tomography (PET), magnetic resonance imaging (MRI), and computed tomography (CT or CAT) allow researchers to study both the structure and function of the brain.

Question: *How can I improve my memory?*

If you have difficulty remembering important information that you need immediately, such as people's names, you can use memory tricks. For instance, when you meet someone, you can attach some funny connotation to that person's name. Mr. Jones has a big nose; therefore, you remember him as Mr. Jonesknows. The semantic strategies mentioned in chapter 6 may also help.

Health food stores offer certain products that claim to aid in memory. One mentioned by the American Medical Association as possibly effective is ginkgo, a tree extract (Le Bars et al., 1997). Although I have had no personal experience with this product, I have met many who use it and believe in it. (You just have to remember to take it!)

Eating well and taking care of yourself are important to memory. Follow the brain diet previously mentioned. The less stress you have in your life, the easier it will be to remember what is important. Also, visual memory is very powerful. As my children grow up, I find myself looking through albums and remembering the "good old days." For your personal memories, keeping a journal and taking photographs may be a great way to relive and revive some great times.

There are tricks that you can use to improve your memory.

Ginkgo, a tree extract, may improve memory.

Lowering your stress level may help your memory.

Question: *I have heard about memory in relation to something called CREB. What is it?*

CREB stands for "cyclic amp-response element binding" protein. Scientists are studying this protein molecule because they believe it may be responsible for long-term memory. Many pharmaceutical companies

The CREB molecule is believed to be responsible for long-term memory.

Many companies are developing memory-enhancing drugs.

determined to find drugs to aid in memory treatment are conducting research on this protein.

One study of fruit flies found that those with a higher level of CREB formed memories more quickly than those with a lower level (Society for Neuroscience, 1997). In fact, the fruit flies learned after only one lesson! Students would definitely benefit if research proves this protein molecule is critical to long-term memory development. Research continues, and many companies have developed memory-enhancing drugs that they hope will help patients with Alzheimer's disease and other forms of dementia. Further research will be required before such drugs are used on children.

Question: *When should new information be introduced in the classroom?*

For students to remember new information, it must be repeated. Monday, Tuesday, and perhaps Wednesday are good days for introducing information. I find that students generally forget any new concept that I introduce on Thursday or Friday. Because of the intervening weekend, they simply have not had enough time to activate long-term memory.

Important information should be presented at the beginning of class.

Because most people remember beginnings and endings better than middle sections, try to present important information at the start of class, work with material through an activity during the middle of the class, and reinforce the concept at the end. The brain can retain incorrect information given at the beginning of a class; so be sure you have presented the new information correctly before seeking student feedback. Unfortunately, misinformation could show up on a test because the brain was so eager to absorb what was presented incorrectly at the opening of the class (Sousa, 1995).

Pre-exposure is a powerful way to help students make connections.

Pre-exposure can be a powerful way to help kids make connections with new material. I make it a habit to go through the table of contents in textbooks with my students. We discuss the topics casually, but this exposure to the material helps them learn it later in the year. Another pre-exposure trick is to hang posters or other information in the room a few weeks before presenting the actual content. The students have some identification with the material, and it does not appear as frightening or new (Jensen, 1996).

Question: *Can music make kids smarter?*

Preschoolers who took music lessons scored higher on spatial-temporal reasoning.

Studies of music and learning have been going on for decades, with some promising results. Gordon Shaw and Frances Rauscher of the University of California at Irvine conducted experiments using the music of Mozart. The results showed that listening to Mozart could increase spatial-temporal IQ. Extending this finding, these researchers then gave preschoolers music lessons. When compared with a group that had not had lessons, these children scored higher on spatial-temporal reasoning—knowing how items fit in space and time. The effects appear to be long-term (Diamond & Hopson, 1998).

Playing music from the Baroque period has been said to increase memory and test-taking skills. This may be a result of the relaxing effect this music has on the body and possibly the brain (Rose, 1985).

When people hear music they like, the experience causes the release of endorphins, which makes them feel good. If a student is in a positive state, it seems natural that learning may take place more easily. In earlier chapters I have suggested some ways to use music. I find it very valuable as a memory aid.

Question: *How do rewards fit into a brain-compatible classroom?*

We would all like our students to be intrinsically motivated. Some of them may be; many are not. By giving tangible rewards to students, you are literally taking away some of that intrinsic motivation. The brain perceives *not* receiving the reward as a punishment. Rewards also seem to limit individual creativity. For example, the student may think, "If I write my essay just like this, I'll get an A. I did it this way the last time I got an A" (Kohn, 1993). Reed Larson of the University of Illinois believes that rewards and punishments take away motivation. The reward itself becomes the focus, and the punishment causes frustration (Diamond & Hopson, 1998).

Positive feedback raises serotonin levels and is itself a reward. We need to talk more with our students and give them the feedback they need. Recognition is more powerful than rewards. Celebrating at the end of a unit gives students an emotional memory that may help motivate them for the next unit. This celebration cannot be based on test results or behavior, however—or it becomes a reward.

Believe me, there are days when I would like to bribe my students to behave or work harder. It has taken me several years to hold back the candy, homework passes, and other rewards. When I place my students on teams and they keep charts for self-assessment, I find they work better and feel better about themselves. Occasionally I have a student who asks me what he will "get" if he scores well. I simply walk up to the student, take his hand, and shake it. The issue is usually dropped.

Question: *Do television and video games help brains grow?*

Watching television does not stimulate brain growth. On the contrary, it may result in loss of neuronal connections. Dendrites will shrivel from lack of use. Both television and video games may be responsible for such loss (Diamond & Hopson, 1998). Brain researchers and child development experts recommend limited amounts of time for either of these

Music that you enjoy will cause the release of endorphins—those feel-good brain chemicals.

Rewards and punishment may diminish motivation.

Celebrations that are not based on behavior or test results are not rewards.

Television watching does not stimulate brain growth.

activities. They also suggest that television viewing be supervised. Although video games may improve eye-hand coordination, they do not replace the need for problem solving, reading, and writing (Healy, 1994).

Question: *Why has brain research become so important?*

Congress and President Bush proclaimed that the 1990s would be the decade of the brain (Society for Neuroscience, 1997). My interest began in the late 1980s as I was desperately trying to figure out what to do with a class. I was looking for answers, and brain research gave me several. Twenty-five years ago there were only about 500 neuroscientists in the United States. Today there are more than 25,000 registered neuroscientists (Society for Neuroscience, 1997). The field has been expanding in part because of incredible new brain-imaging and testing techniques.

Doctors have always been interested in the brain, but until recently their methods of discovery were very limited. Usually, they had to use cadavers and autopsy to find out anything. They would monitor patients with certain problems and, after death, dissect the brain; based on the patients' symptoms, they would then figure out which area was damaged. From this information they slowly discovered approximately which areas of the brain controlled certain functions. It was a slow and often disappointing process. Now so many kinds of research are going on that the field needs more neuroscientists.

Much of this new study has produced astonishing results. Researchers are beginning to understand brain development. They have identified many areas of the brain that contribute to learning and memory. The discovery of how the brain compensates for loss and damage has been enlightening and promising for those with brain disease. This plasticity, the ability of the brain to change, means that IQ can change throughout life. The idea of enriched environments has affected parents, teachers, schools, and day care centers. We now have information available that can make a difference in everyone's life.

The Internet puts much information about the brain at our fingertips. Sites for children are also available, such as the following World Wide Web resources:

- *Neuroscience for Kids:* http://weber.u.washington.edu/~chudler/neurok.html
- *Jay's Brain:* http://www.exn.net/Main/JaysBrain/archives.cfm
- *Mind Over Matter:* http://www.nida.nih.gov/MOM/TG/momtg-index.html

(Note: Web site addresses change frequently, so be sure to do some searches of your own.)

Sidebar notes:

Today there are more than 25,000 registered neuroscientists.

Brain-imaging techniques have changed the way scientists can look at the brain.

IQ can change throughout life.

The futurists tell us that information is doubling at accelerated rates. Learning everything is impossible. What has become as important as learning content is learning how best to learn. Our children must understand their own learning needs so they can learn what is necessary at different times in their lives. Brain research is giving us this information. We are a long way from knowing it all, but we are getting closer every day.

Question: *How can I start making my classroom brain compatible?*

You have many options. You can use multiple intelligences, learning styles, or the memory lanes to begin. These will make your teaching more brain compatible. Decide which of these will best fit your teaching style. If you decide to make changes after school has already begun, go slowly. Your students have become accustomed to your style of teaching and the structure in your classroom. Their brains will shift down to survival level if you change too much at once.

I began using brain-compatible strategies after a summer of training and researching. I am the type of person who jumps into things quickly, and it worked well for me. I created colorful posters and decorated my room with positive affirmations. I replaced all of the white chalk with colored chalk to make using the chalkboard more fun and appealing. I studied the uses of music and put together a collection that I wanted to use during the year. I planned to put my students in teams and decided how to form the teams and assess them. I set goals for myself and made plans for my students to set goals. I looked at the units of study I would cover and decided how to access the memory lanes. I developed assessments that I felt would tell me what my students had learned through those lanes. I began teaching in a multimodal fashion, making sure that every lesson contained a visual, an auditory, and a kinesthetic component. These were some external changes that I made. They could be accomplished within a school year by making a few changes at a time.

I had to make some internal changes as well. I knew I could no longer be the focal point in my class. I began to look at my students as teachers and treat them that way, too. I became a facilitator. That was a new role for me. I liked it. My students became little brains with dendrites searching for learning and meaning. I felt as though I had a much more important job than just teaching a curriculum.

Question: *First I was trained in learning styles; then I took a class in multiple intelligences (which by the way, they keep adding to—are there eight or nine now?); and now you want me to look at these memory lanes. What am I supposed to do? There are too many things for me to think about in one class period!*

Whenever I am asked this question, I think about my own teaching schedule and understand exactly what a burden and responsibility all of

Information is doubling at enormous rates. We must learn how to learn.

Make changes in your classroom slowly.

Make learning appealing.

Look at your students as teachers, too.

Teachers make hundreds of decisions each day.

Choose strategies that you are comfortable with.

Educators have been seeking research with classroom applications.

Brain research is here to stay!

this may be. I have trouble remembering my ID number so I can eat in the cafeteria, my calling card number so I can call my children at school, and the grading scale! Now, let's see. There are currently 8 intelligences, 22 elements of one of the learning style programs, and 5 memory lanes. I opted for the lowest number—5.

Seriously, using any of these approaches to your teaching will probably be quite brain friendly. Howard Gardner's (1993) multiple intelligence theory is brain-based. Research suggests that learning styles are as well (Given, 1997). Choose whatever will work best for you. Teachers need to believe in what they are trying to do. I have used techniques related to learning styles in my classroom since the 1980s. It has become my way of thinking whenever I put lessons together. I began adopting the memory lane strategies in the past several years as I became more involved in memory research. It works for me. I also use the multiple intelligence theory at various times throughout the year. Whatever approach you choose will still allow you to incorporate the other approaches.

Question: *Is brain research just another fad?*

Brain research is not new. For at least the last 25 years educators have been seeking research that translates into practical application in the classroom. The first brain-research theory I was ever introduced to was the right/left brain theory (Hooper & Teresi, 1986). It was different and exciting at the time. Shortly after that, I read about the triune brain theory and became excited about its implications for education (Healy, 1994). Now there are hundreds of theories, but not too many that we can apply to classroom instruction. Neuroscientists are not pursuing research that can be applied to teaching. However, many of us have put some brain theories to the test and have obtained positive results in the classroom. It is going to take this on-the-job training and research to discover what will work.

Brain research and brain-compatible methods have stood the test of time. That is what usually determines value and credibility. Brain research is here to stay. It is giving validity to the successful methods that have worked for years, and it is uncovering new information that will change the way we teach and the way students learn for decades to come.

Glossary

acetylcholine—neurotransmitter involved in muscle movement and memory

action potential—signal sent down the axon of a neuron when the neuron is stimulated

adrenaline—hormone released from the adrenal gland during stress; also called epinephrine

amino acids—fast-acting neurotransmitters that include GABA and glutamate

amygdala—forebrain structure that catalogs emotional memory

antidepressant—drug used to balance availability of neurotransmitters in the brain

association cortex—area of the cerebral cortex responsible for processing information

authentic assessment—assessment associated with a real-life task

automatic memory—reflexive memory located in the cerebellum

axon—part of the neuron that sends the signal to another neuron

brain stem—lower part of the brain where information enters

Broca's area—area in the frontal lobe that puts spoken words in order

catecholamines—neurotransmitters such as norepinephrine, epinephrine, and dopamine; a type of monoamine

cell membrane—outer covering of the brain cell or neuron

cerebellum—hindbrain structure responsible for balance and posture; contains procedural and automatic memories

cerebrum—forebrain structure that contains mostly myelinated axon fibers

corpus callosum—large band of fibers connecting the two hemispheres of the brain

cortisol—stress chemical released by the adrenal gland that can damage the hippocampus

CREB (cyclic amp-response element binding)—molecule believed to be associated with long-term memory

dendrite—neuronal structure that receives signals from sending neurons

dopamine—neurotransmitter associated with movement and pleasure

emotional memory—memory filed in the amygdala that deals with feelings

endorphin—endogenous morphine; the body's natural pain killer

epinephrine—another term for adrenaline

episodic memory—location-oriented memories filed in the hippocampus

excitatory neurotransmitter—chemical that causes neurons to fire

explicit memory—type of memory associated with the hippocampus that involves memories of words, facts, and places

forebrain—large part of the brain containing the cerebral hemispheres, hippocampus, amygdala, thalamus, hypothalamus, pituitary gland, and pineal gland

frontal lobe—the part of the front of the brain that is involved in critical thinking, problem solving, planning, and decision making

GABA (gamma-aminobutyric acid)—very prevalent inhibitory neurotransmitter

glial cell—brain cell that nurtures neurons

glutamate—very prevalent excitatory neurotransmitter

hindbrain—lower area of the brain that includes the brain stem, medulla oblongata, and pons

hippocampus—structure located in the forebrain that catalogs long-term factual memories

hypothalamus—structure located in the forebrain

that regulates and sorts internal information

implicit memory—involuntary memory such as the procedural, emotional, and automatic memories

indoleamines—neurotransmitters such as serotonin and melatonin; a type of monoamine

inhibitory neurotransmitter—brain chemical that prevents neurons from firing

ion—atom that is charged in the brain, such as potassium and sodium

limbic system—area of the brain associated with emotions and memory

long-term memory—process by which the brain stores information for long periods of time

long-term potentiation (LTP)—process by which neural networks are strengthened quickly

magnetic resonance imaging (MRI)—brain-imaging technique using a large magnetic field to map the structure of the brain

mammalian brain—limbic area of the brain

melatonin—neurotransmitter associated with the wake/sleep cycle

midbrain—small area of the brain associated with vision

mnemonics—devices to make semantic learning easier

monoamines—group of neurotransmitters divided into two classes: catecholamines and indoleamines

myelin—fatty substance that coats most axons for smoother and faster transmission of messages

neocortex—upper layer of the cerebrum, about one-eighth-inch thick, where higher thinking takes place

neural pruning—removal of synapses that are unused

neurohormone—chemical released by the brain that affects the body

neuron—brain cell associated with learning and memory

neuroscientist—scientist who studies the function and structure of the brain

neurotransmitter—chemical produced in a neuron that carries information in the brain

norepinephrine—neurotransmitter associated with alertness

occipital lobe—part of the brain, located at the rear of the cerebrum, where vision is processed

parietal lobe—part of the brain located on the top of the cerebrum that receives sensation from the body in the form of pain, pressure, temperature, and touch

peptides—hormones that travel throughout the body carrying messages

performance assessment—demonstration of a behavior that is evaluated using a rubric

pineal gland—gland that regulates the release of neurotransmitters that regulate sleep

pituitary gland—gland that runs the endocrine system

positron emission tomography (PET)—brain-imaging technique that measures the amount of glucose consumed by areas of the brain while subjects perform various activities

reptilian brain—brain stem

resting potential—voltage of a neuron when it is not being stimulated

reticular activating system (RAS)—system that regulates the amount and flow of information entering the brain

semantic memory—word memory

serotonin—neurotransmitter that causes relaxation and affects mood

short-term memory—memory that lasts only seconds

synapse—space between the axon of a sending neuron and the dendrite or receptor site of the receiving neuron

temporal lobe—part of the brain located on the sides of the cerebrum that is responsible for hearing, speech, and some learning and memory

thalamus—forebrain structure, part of the limbic system, that sorts incoming information

triune brain—model of the brain developed by Dr.

Paul Maclean in which the brain is thought of as three systems

vesicles—storage areas for neurotransmitters within the neuron

Wernicke's area—area located in the temporal lobe that changes thoughts and sounds into words

working memory—process that takes place in the frontal lobes in which information is temporarily stored until either stored in long-term memory or dropped

Bibliography

Baddeley, A. (1990). *Human memory*. Boston: Allyn & Bacon.

Begley, S. (1997, Spring/Summer). How to build a baby's brain. *Newsweek* [special edition], 28–32.

Caine, R. N., & Caine, G. (1994). *Making connections: Teaching and the human brain*. Menlo Park, CA: Addison-Wesley.

Calvin, W. H., & Ojemann, G. A. (1994). *Conversations with Neil's brain*. Reading, MA: Addison-Wesley.

Chudler, E. (1998, April 24). Do we use only 10% of our brain? In *Neuroscience Resources for Kids* [On-line]. Available: http://weber.u.washington.edu/~chudler/tenper.html

Cohen, D. (1996). *The secret language of the mind*. San Francisco: Chronicle Books.

Diamond, M. (Speaker). (1996). *The brain, the mind, and the classroom* (Cassette Recording). Alexandria, VA: Association for Supervision and Curriculum Development.

Diamond, M., & Hopson, J. (1998). *Magic trees of the mind*. New York: Dutton.

Diamond, M., Scheibel, A., Murphy, G., and Harvey, T. (1985). On the brain of a scientist: Albert Einstein. *Experimental Neurology, 88*, 198–204.

Diamond, M. C. (1988). *Enriching heredity: The impact of the environment on the anatomy of the brain*. New York: Free Press.

Dowling, J. E. (1998). *Creating mind*. New York: W. W. Norton.

Engelkamp, J., & Zimmer, H. D. (1994). *The human memory: A multi-modal approach*. Seattle: Hogrefe & Huber.

Fitzpatrick, S. (Speaker). (1996). *The brain, the mind, and the classroom* (Cassette Recording). Alexandria, VA: Association for Supervision and Curriculum Development.

Gardner, H. (1993). *Frames of mind: The theory of multiple intelligences*. New York: Basic Books.

Given, B. (1997). The neurobiology of learning style. *The Brain Based Education/Learning Styles Networker, 10*, 5, 7.

Glasser, W. (1986). *Control theory in the classroom*. New York: Perennial Library.

Glenn, H. S. (1990). *The greatest human need* (Video Recording). Gold River, CA: Capabilities, Inc.

Golden, D. (1994, July). Brain calisthenics. *Life, 11*, 62.

Goleman, D. (1995). *Emotional intelligence*. New York: Bantam.

Grinder, M. (1991). *Righting the educational conveyor belt*. Portland, OR: Metamorphous Press.

Hannaford, C. (1995). *Smart moves*. Arlington, VA: Great Oceans Publishers.

Hart, L. A. (1983). *Human brain and human learning*. New York: Longman.

Healy, J. (1990). *Endangered minds: Why children don't think and what we can do about it*. New York: Simon & Schuster.

Healy, J. (1994). *Your child's growing mind*. New York: Doubleday.

Hobson, J. A. (1994). *The chemistry of conscious states*. Boston: Little, Brown, & Co.

Hooper, J., & Teresi, D. (1986). *The three-pound universe*. Los Angeles: J. P. Tarcher.

Howard, P. (1994). *The owner's manual for the brain*. Austin, TX: Leornian Press.

Jensen, E. (1995). *Brain-based learning & teaching*. Del Mar, CA: Turning Point Publishing.

Jensen, E. (1996). *Completing the puzzle: The brain-based approach*. Del Mar, CA: Turning Point Publishing.

Jensen, E. (1998). *Teaching with the brain in mind*. Alexandria, VA: Association for Supervision and Curriculum Development.

Jourdain, R. (1997). *Music, the brain, and ecstasy*. New York: W. Morrow.

Khalsa, D. S. (1997). *Brain longevity*. New York: Warner Books.

Kinoshita, J. (1999, January/February). Replenishing the brain's neurons. *Brainworks: The Neuroscience Newsletter, 9*, 1–2.

Kohn, A. (1993). *Punished by rewards*. Boston: Houghton Mifflin.

Kotulak, R. (1996). *Inside the brain*. Kansas City, MO: Andrews & McMeel.

Kunzig, R. (1998, August). Climbing through the brain. *Discover, 19*, 61–69.

Le Bars, P. L., Katz, M. M., Berman, N., Itil, T. M., Freedman, A. M., Schatzberg, A. F., & North American EGb Study Group. (1997, October 22). Placebo-controlled double-blind randomized trial of an extract of Ginkgo biloba for dementia. *Journal of the American Medical Association* [On-line], *54*. Available: http://www.ama-assn.org/sci-pubs/journals/archive/jama/vol_278/no_16/toc.htm

LeDoux, J. E. (1996). *The emotional brain*. New York: Simon & Schuster.

Leiner, H., & Leiner, A. (1997, September). The treasure at the bottom of the brain. *The Brain Lab* [On-line]. Available: http://www.newhorizons.org/blab_leiner.html

Lemonick, M. (1997, September 29). The mood molecule. *Time, 150*, 74–82.

Margulies, N., & Sylwester, R. (1998). *Memory*. Tucson, AZ: Zephyr Press.

Mark, V., & Mark, J. (1989). *Brain power*. Boston: Houghton Mifflin.

Nash, J. M. (1997, February 3). Fertile minds. *Time, 149*, 48–56.

Neville, H. (1997, January). Old brain/new tricks. *Ask the Scientists* [On-line]). Available: http://www.pbs.org/saf/3_ask/33_interview_neville.html

Pert, C. B. (1997). *Molecules of emotion*. New York: Scribner.

Pinker, S. (1997) *How the mind works*. New York: W. W. Norton & Co.

Posner, M., & Raichle, M. (1997). *Images of mind*. New York: Scientific American Library.

Restak, R. M. (1994). *Receptors*. New York: Bantam Books.

Restak, R. M. (1995). *Brainscapes*. New York: Hyperion.

Rose, C. (1985). *Accelerated learning*. New York: Dell Publishing.

Rose, C. P., & Nicholl, M. J. (1997). *Accelerated learning for the 21st century*. New York: Delacourt Press.

Rose, S. P. R. (1993). *The making of memory*. New York: Anchor Books.

Rosenzweig, M., & Bennett, R. (1972). Cerebral changes in rats, exposed individually to an enriched environment. *Journal of Comparative and Physical Psychology, 80*, 304–313.

Sapolsky, R. (1994). *Why zebras don't get ulcers*. New York: W.H. Freeman.

Society for Neuroscience. (1997). About the society for neuroscience [On-line]. Available: http://www.sfn.org/

Sousa, D. (1995). *How your brain learns*. Reston, VA: NASSP.

Sylwester, R. (1995). *A celebration of neurons*. Alexandria, VA: Association for Supervision and Curriculum Development.

Sylwester, R. (Speaker). (1997a). *Recent educationally significant developments in memory* (Cassette Recording). Alexandria, VA: Association for Supervision and Curriculum Development.

Sylwester, R. (Speaker). (1997b). *Applying brain stress research to classroom management* (Cassette Recording). Alexandria, VA: Association for Supervision and Curriculum Development.

Sylwester, R. (1997c, February). The neurobiology of self-esteem and aggression. *Educational Leadership, 54*, 75–79.

Wilson, M. A., & McNaughton, B. L. (1994). Reactivation of hippocampal ensemble memories during sleep. *Science, 265*, 676–679.

Wolfe, P. (Speaker). (1996). *Translating brain research into practice* (Cassette Recording). Alexandria, VA: Association for Supervision and Curriculum Development.

Wurtman, J. J. (1986). *Managing your mind and mood through food*. New York: Perennial Library.

Wurtman, J., & Suffes, S. (1996). *The serotonin solution: The potent brain chemical that can help you stop bingeing, lose weight, and feel great*. New York: Fawcett Columbine.

Index

acetylcholine, 23–24, 96
acronyms, 69–70
acrostics, 70
action potential, 10
activity, impact on IQ, 13–14
addictive substances, brain activity and, 17
adolescents, brains of, 96
adrenal glands, response to stress, 39
Alzheimer's disease, 98
amino acids, 20–21
amygdala, 34, 36(fig), 37
  development of, 55
  effect of stress on, 54
  emotional memory and, 54, 62
  response to stress, 39, 55(fig)
antidepressants, 16, 23
appetite control, 37
assessments of memory, 82–87, 88–89
  matching to types of memory, 83–87
  performance, 83
  portfolio, 82–83
  teaching to the test, 88–89
association cortex, 50
attention
  factors affecting, 95
  keeping, 94–95
attention-getters, 95
auditory information, 38, 48, 49
authentic assessment, 83
automatic memory, 35, 46, 50, 53–54, 55(fig), 60(fig)
  assessment of, 85–86
  instructional strategies for, 75, 89
axons, 2, 3(fig), 4(fig)
  action potential and, 10
  myelin coating around, 6(fig)
  neurotransmitters and, 16

Baddeley, Alan, 48
balance, 35
behavior, influence of neurotransmitters on, 25–28
brain
  anatomy of, 34(fig), 34–41
  electrical power in, 8, 9
  examining hemispheres of, 41–43
  lobes of, 42–43, 43(fig)
  maturation process of, 31
  memory pathways in, 46
  passage of information through, 38
  response to stress, 38–39
  triune model of, 32–33
brain cells, 1–8
  axons, 2–6
  glial cells, 5
  myelin, 5–8
  neurons, 2–5
brain chemicals, number of, 16
brain growth, 96
  effect of stress on, 12–13
  encouraged by activity, 13, 14
  myelin release and, 7(fig)
  television and video game effect on, 99–100
brain research, 100, 102
brain stem, 32(fig), 32–33, 34, 35, 35(fig), 38, 50
Broca's area, 42
bulletin boards, in the classroom, 73, 77, 84

calpain, 96
carbohydrates, 95, 96
catecholamines, 21
CAT scan, 96–97
cat studies, 13
cell body, 2, 3(fig)
cerebellum
  information storage and access in, 74, 85
  role in automatic memory, 53
  role in procedural memory, 34, 35, 35(fig), 52, 55(fig)
  role in storing kinesthetic information, 49–50

Note: Index references with (fig) indicate that information is found in a figure on that page.

cerebral cortex, 38
cerebrum, 34, 36(fig), 38
channels, 9, 9(fig)
chemical imbalances, 27–28
chemical messages, 3, 25
child development stages, 6–7, 7(fig)
"chunking" of information, 70. *See also* short-term
    memory
classroom environments
    making brain compatible, 101
    methods of affecting neurotransmitters in, 25
    as positive factor in affecting brain chemistry, 28–29
computed tomography, 97
concrete operation (child development stage), 7, 7(fig)
conditioned response memory, 53
conscious memory, 46
contextual memory, 51
corpus callosum, 36(fig), 38, 41, 42
cortisol, 24, 27–28
    blocking of factual memory, 56
    response to stress, 39, 40, 54
cramming, 49, 51
CREB (cyclic amp-response element binding), 97–98
critical periods, 93

debates, 67
decision-making, 5–8, 26, 33. *See also* higher-order
    thinking skills
declarative memory, 46
dendrites, 2, 3(fig), 4(fig)
    action potential and, 10
    growth of, 10–14
    neurotransmitters and, 16
dendritic growth
    encouraged by enriched environments, 11, 12(fig)
    related to activity, 11–12
depression, as imbalance in brain chemistry, 26
developmental stages of children, 8
Diamond, Marian, 11–13
diet. *See also* food, effect on brain
    as aid to learning, 95
    good for brain, 96
dopamine, 21, 22
    diet and, 96
    effect on behavior, 25

"downshifting," 40–41
dramatic performances, 76

early environment, effect on brain, 13
Einstein, Albert, brain of, 5
electrical messages, 2–3
emotional development, 94
"emotional hijacking," 31
emotional information, importance of amygdala to,
    37–38
Emotional Intelligence (Goleman), 41
emotional intelligence, impact of, 41
emotional memory, 61
    assessment of, 86–87
    and hippocampus development, 46, 50, 54–55,
        55(fig), 56, 60(fig), 62
    instructional strategies for, 75–76, 89
    used to enhance learning, 65
emotions, 33
    effect on learning, 43–44, 95
    primacy of, 41, 54, 60, 87
endocrine system, 37
endogenous morphine. *See* endorphin
endorphin, 24, 25, 99
enriched environments, 11–13, 14, 100
epinephrine, 21, 24
episodic memory, 46, 50, 51–52, 55(fig), 56, 59,
    60(fig), 61
    assessment of, 84
    as "dangerous," 56
    instructional strategies for, 73–74, 76, 77, 89
excitatory neurotransmitters, 16–17, 20, 21
explicit memory, 50

fat, effects on brain, 18, 24
fetal development, 5, 31, 96
"fight or flight" response, 27, 39
flash cards, 75, 77
food, effect on brain, 17–18, 24, 95, 96
forebrain, 34, 34(fig), 36(fig), 36–38
formal operations (child development stage), 7, 7(fig)
frontal lobes, 42, 43(fig)
functional MRI (fMRI), 46, 97

GABA, 20–21

gamma-aminobutyric acid. *See* GABA
Gardner, Howard, 102
gingko, 97
glial, 5
glial cells, 5
glutamate, 20–21
Goleman, Daniel, 31, 41, 54
graphic organizers, 65–66
Greenough, William, 11

Hannaford, Carla, 5, 8
Healy, Jane, 5, 7
hemispheres of the brain, 37, 41–43
higher-order thinking skills, 6–8, 32(fig), 66
  as developmental, 6–7, 7(fig)
  difficulty with, 7–8
  limbic brain as stepping stone toward, 33
  neocortex as location of, 33
  prefrontal lobe and, 42
hindbrain, 34–35, 34(fig)
hippocampus, 2, 34, 36(fig), 37
  and episodic memory, 52
  late development of, 55
  response to stress, 39, 40
  role in episodic memory, 52, 55(fig), 59
  role in semantic memory, 50–51, 59
  role in storing explicit memory, 50
homeostasis, 37
hypothalamus, 34, 36(fig), 37

implicit memory, 50
indoleamines, 21, 22–23
information
  passage through brain, 38
  processing of, 50
inhibitory neurotransmitters, 16–17, 20–21, 22
instructional strategies. *See also* classroom
  environments
    automatic memory, 75, 89
    emotional memory, 75–76, 89
    episodic memory, 73–74, 76, 77, 89
    procedural memory, 74–75, 89
    semantic memory, 65–71, 76, 77, 89
    success of listeners vs. memorizers, 90–91
    teams, 25, 72, 101

Internet, 100
introducing new information, 98
"invisible information," 52, 84
involuntary systems, 34–35
ions, makeup of, 8–9
IQ, 13–14, 100

jet lag, 23
journal keeping, 87

kinesthetic information, 48, 49

language arts, 72, 75. *See also* oral presentations and
  classwork, reading, writing
language development, 41–42, 93–94
Larson, Reed, 99
L-dopa, 22
learning
  defined by neuroscientists, 2
  environmental effect on, 8
  lobe development and, 43
  love of, by students, 82
  made more powerful by memory, 60–61, 62–63, 64
  memory and, 46–47
  and play, 14
  as social activity, 14
learning styles, 70, 101–102
LeDoux, Joseph, 48
life span
  effect of gentle care on, 12–13, 14
  effect of stress on, 12–13
limbic area, 34, 36, 41
limbic brain, 32(fig), 33
location, episodic memory and, 72–74, 84
long-term memory, 23, 40, 48, 49–55, 91, 94. *See also*
  hippocampus
long-term potentiation (LTP), 4

Maclean, Paul, 32–33
magnetic resonance imaging (MRI), 46, 97
mammalian brain. *See* limbic brain
math, 52, 74, 75, 82–83, 84
medulla oblongata, 35, 35(fig)
melatonin, 21, 23, 37
memories, making, 57–59, 59–60

memory. *See also* automatic memory, conditioned re-
    sponse memory, conscious memory, contextual mem-
    ory, declarative memory, emotional memory, episodic
    memory, explicit memory, implicit memory, long-
    term memory, muscle memory, procedural memory,
    semantic memory, short-term memory, spatial mem-
    ory, working memory
        assessment of, 82–87
        effects of, 62–63
        importance of hippocampus to, 37, 38
        interaction between types of, 54
        learning and, 46–47, 63
        improving, 97
        multiple lanes of, 49–55, 76–80
        overcoming failure of, 61–62
        pruning of, 60
        role of cerebellum in formation, 35
        triggering of, 53–54
memory lanes, location of, 55(fig)
Memory (Marguiles and Sylwester), 90
memory retrieval, designing tests for, 89
midbrain, 34, 34(fig), 35(fig), 36
Miller, George, 48
mind mapping, 65, 88, 94
mnemonic devices, 68–70
monoamines, 20, 21–24
motor cortex, as storage for kinesthetic information,
    49–50
motor strip, 43(fig)
movement, 8, 35, 75
Mozart, 98
MRI, 46, 96–97
multiple intelligences, 101–102
muscle memory, 35, 52, 75
music, 24
    effect on intelligence, 98–99
    as means to enhance memory, 75, 76, 86
    as trigger for memories, 59, 60
    as trigger for release of positive chemicals, 25
myelin, 5–8, 6(fig), 43
myelination, 5–6, 8

neocortex, 3, 32(fig), 33, 34, 36(fig), 38, 39, 41
neural hijacking, 54
neural network, 3–4

neural pruning, 2
neurohormones, 16
neuronal connections
    in early development, 4
    pruning of, 56
neurons, 2–5
    active, 10(fig)
    auditory, 31
    communication between, 2, 4(fig)
    depiction of, 3(fig)
    during fetal development, 31
    effect of environment on, 12(fig)
    electrical and chemical activity of, 17(fig)
    enriched, 12(fig)
    firing of, 18–19
    impoverished, 12(fig)
    information transfer and myelin, 8
    language development and, 93–94
    learning and, 47
    neurotransmitters and, 16
    number produced, 2
    parts of, 2–4
    resting, 9(fig)
    transmissions between, 16, 17(fig)
    transmissions within, 16, 17(fig)
    visual, 31
    with myelin, 6(fig)
neuron signals, 8–10
    action potential, 10
    resting potential, 9
neuroscience, growth of, 100
neurotransmitters, 3, 16
    behavior and, 25–28
    classes of, 16–17, 21(fig)
    diet and, 96
    effects on feelings and actions, 18–28
    formation and action of, 19
    imbalance in, 26
    negative attention as stimulus for, 28
    operation of, 16–20
    regulated by pineal gland, 37
    storage and movement of, 20(fig)
    types of, 20–24
newborns, 93–94
norepinephrine, 21, 27

diet and, 96
   effect on behavior, 25
   role in focusing attention, 95
novelty, 95
nuns, studies of longevity in, 13
nursing homes, studies of residents' IQ, 13–14

occipital lobe, 42, 43(fig), 49
opiate receptors, 24
oral presentations and classwork, 40, 60–61, 75, 85–86
outlining, 67

pain killer, endorphin as, 24
paraphrasing, 68
parietal lobes, 42, 43(fig)
peer teaching, 66, 88, 94
peg system, 68–69, 69(fig), 70(fig), 88
peptides, 16, 20, 24, 39
performance assessment, 83
PET scan, 96–97. See positron emission tomography
Piaget, Jean, 6–7
pineal gland, 36(fig), 37
pituitary gland, 36(fig), 37, 39
plasticity, 10–11
play and learning, 14
pons, 34–35, 35(fig)
portfolio assessment, 82–83
positive feedback, 25, 26, 99
positron emission tomography (PET) scans, 46, 94,
   96–97
powerful learning, 60–61, 64
power pictures, 65, 66(fig), 88
practice tests, 67–68
prefrontal cortex, 55(fig)
   role in semantic memory, 5
   role in working memory, 48
prefrontal lobe, 42
pre-operational stage (child development), 6, 7(fig)
problem-solving, 41, 42, 67, 100. See also higher-order
   thinking skills
procedural memory, 35, 46, 50, 52–53, 55(fig), 59–60,
   60(fig), 61
   assessment of, 85
   instructional strategies for, 74–75, 89
protein, 18, 96

pruning, 2, 56, 60, 94
questioning strategies, 66
quiz shows, as instructional strategies, 75

Ramey, Craig, 13
RAS. See reticular activating system
rat studies, 11–13
Rauscher, Frances, 98
reading, 8, 33, 59, 77–79, 100
REM (rapid eye movement), 51
repetition, importance of, 74–75
reptilian brain. See brain stem
resting potential, 9
reticular activating system (RAS), 34, 35(fig), 36, 39
retirement, 25–27
reuptake, 20, 22
rewards, 99
right-brain/left-brain orientation, 41
role-playing, 67, 76, 86, 88
"runner's high," 24

science, 74, 85
semantic information and questioning, 66
semantic memory, 46, 50, 50–51, 55(fig), 59, 60(fig),
   61
   assessment of, 87
   instructional strategies for, 65–71, 76, 77, 89
sensorimotor information, 34
sensorimotor stage (child development), 6, 7(fig)
sensory information, 36
sensory strip, 42, 43(fig)
serotonin, 18, 21, 27–28, 96
   effect on behavior, 25, 26
   lack of, 23
   operation of, 22–23
   positive feedback and, 99
   reuptake, 22–23
sexual function, 37
Shaw, Gordon, 98
short-term memory, 46, 48–49
   brain location of, 7
   buffers, 48, 55(fig)
   limitations of, 48
sleep, information processing during, 51
Sousa, David, 48

spatial memory, 51
spatial-temporal IQ, 98–99
specific serotonin reuptake inhibitors. *See* SSRI
split-brain surgery, 42
SSRI, 23
stimulus-response effects, 35
storytelling, 76–77
stress
    downshifting and, 40–41
    effect on amygdala, 54
    effect on brain growth and life span, 12–13
    negative effect on retrieving memory, 62
    negative physical effects of, 24
    reducing, in the classroom, 28–29
    response to, 38–39, 43
    triggered by test anxiety, 91
students. *See also* developmental stages
    adolescent, 96
    and attention, 54, 95–95
    behavior of, 25–28
    and celebrations, 76, 99
    creating mnemonic devices, 68–70
    and creativity, 12, 77–79
    engaging of, 77, 94–95
    and love of learning, 82
    and need for novelty, 74
    operating from a concrete developmental level, 43,
        44
    operating from a stress response, 40–41, 43
    and peer teaching, 66
    and powerful learning, 60–61, 64
    and rewards, 99
    and rich environments, 12, 28
    at risk, 28
    and teams, 25, 72, 101
    and tests, 49, 51, 64, 67–68, 88–89. *See also*
        assessment, teaching to the test, test anxiety
    transfer, 27
    and understanding of the brain. *See* triune brain

model
summarizing, 67
survival, 33
synapse, 2, 4(fig), 17(fig)
    action potential and, 10
    neurotransmitters and, 16
    pruning of, 94
    strengthening, 17

teaching. *See also* instructional strategies, learning.
    approaches to, 101–102
    to multiple memory lanes, 63
    to the test, 88–89
teaching styles, 79–80
teams, 25, 72, 101
television, 51, 99
temporal lobes, 42, 43(fig), 49
test anxiety, 91–92
testing
    designing for memory lanes, 89–91
    traditional means of, 82, 87
thalamus, 34, 36, 36(fig), 38
    response to stress, 39
    role in semantic memory, 50
    visual information and, 42
time lines, 67
triune brain model, 32–33, 32(fig)
tryptophan, 96
tyrosine, 96

video games, 99
visual information, 38, 42, 48, 49

water, importance to brain function, 96
webbing, 65
Wernicke's area, 42
windows of opportunity, 93–94
working memory, 46, 48–49, 51, 55(fig)
writing, 28, 68, 85, 87, 91, 100

About the Author

Marilee Sprenger is a middle school teacher in Peoria, Illinois. She has a master's degree in curriculum and instruction and since 1992 has spent her summers and weekends training teachers and administrators in brain research and brain-compatible teaching strategies. Sprenger is a member of the American Academy of Neurology and is an adjunct professor at Aurora University. She has co-authored two books, *Powerfully Simple Techniques* and *The Parent Connection*. She speaks at state and national conferences on learning and memory.

You can reach her at 5820 Briarwood Lane, Peoria, IL 61614. Phone: (309) 692-5820. E-mail: msprenge@aol.com (Note that there is no *r* at the end of her e-mail username.)